Rags to Righteousness

Bridget Johnson

Published by Hear My Heart Publishing

Copyright © 2017 Bridget Johnson

All rights reserved. No part of this book may be reproduced or transmitted in any form or by any electronic or mechanical means, including photocopying, recording, or by any information storage and retrieval system, without the written permission of the publisher, except where permitted by law.

Scripture quotations marked (NIV) are taken from the Holy Bible, New International Version®, NIV®. Copyright © 1973, 1978, 1984, 2011 by Biblica, Inc.™ Used by permission of Zondervan. All rights reserved worldwide. www.zondervan.com The "NIV" and "New International Version" are trademarks registered in the United States Patent and Trademark Office by Biblica, Inc.™

ISBN: 978-1-945620-18-8

A product of the United States of America.
Cover design by Lynn Mohney

Acknowledgements

I want to thank my very best friend and my gift from heaven, Ann, for being such an intricate part of my life. She was there with me through the good and the bad times.

I praise God for Peter, my God-ordained spouse; my husband to whom I was called to marry. We, too, have lived a lot of life and I look forward to many more years together.

Denise, my dear friend, is my new traveling companion and my fierce supporter. She has walked this journey with me since we met at work. We enjoy going to conferences together and she is a poster child for my company, Casting Your Vision, LLC. She was 59 years old and didn't believe she had a calling in her life or that it was of any value at all. We started listening to Terri Savelle Foy's teachings on dreams and goals and she lit up. We went to Terri's Next Conference in January 2016 and Denise found out she does have a call and purpose for her life.

There are so many other people that I need to thank and mention. I sometimes tease my dear friend, Michelle, and tell her she was my "fake daughter-in-law" for the child I never had. Thank you, Michelle, for being my supporter and my Christian sister.

Thank you to everyone that have prayed and interceded for me over the years. Thank you to the women that mentored me and watched over me. Thank you to the women who would tell me to stop being emotional and suck it up. Thank you to the pastors of my church in California, Pastor & Mrs. Hagin, and all the teachers at Rhema. Thank you also to my Rhema roommate, Laurie, for suffering with me for two years while we were in school.

To Rick & Lory, thank you so much for being my dear

friends. When I was sad and lonely you were there to be my fun and yes, you had to be tough on me on many occasions. You are my family and you're always there for me.

Table of Contents

Foreword

How it All Began	1
My Mother	8
My Early Days	15
Grandma's House	19
Growing Up Years	21
Our "Church" Life	23
Forced to Grow Up Too Fast	27
Okay, Off the Soapbox Now	32
Finally, My God-Sized Hole Can Get Filled Up	42
My Dear Friend Ann and Our Church Home	53
Dear God, I'm Divorced	60
Hillbilly Trip to Oklahoma	72
Life at Rhema	77
Life After Rhema	81
There is a Purpose	87
Dreams and Goals	89
Letter to the Reader	96

Foreword

I am so happy that you picked up this book. I know you were drawn to it by the wooing of the Holy Spirit. Only the God of heaven and the Savior of the world could draw you to someone who is a virtual unknown. I may be unknown to you. But I'm not unknown to Him.

I did not have an earthly Father that I could count on. My biological Father, as you will read, was no more than someone that had a relationship with my mother. My dad that I called "daddy" who raised me, was a sick alcoholic who didn't know how to love anyone, especially himself.

There was a commercial when I was growing up that was about dog food. The dog food commercial talked about how 'my dog is bigger and better than your dog' because my dog eats this good food. I took that commercial to heart and used to think my dad was bigger than your dad; my dad will come and save me from all the pains of the earth. My dad could beat up your dad…. In reality that wasn't true at all. My dad was usually nowhere to be found and I knew for sure he couldn't beat up anybody else's dad. I never verbalized those words but they were true.

As I write this, I am 56 years old. The scars and pain from 50 years ago are still present.

I had a God-sized hole in my heart that I tried to fill up with everything but God. The things with which I did, to fill it up caused physical harm and heartache; not only for me but for my family. Because of that giant crevice in my soul, I hurt a lot of people. I never had the kind of relationship with my mother, brother or sister that I wanted. I take the blame for my behavior because I was the one acting out. I was the one getting drunk, having sex, and running away from home. I'm the one that did it because <u>no one</u> told me there was a better way.

Religion is not the answer. The stone and wooden gods are not the answer. The answer is a relationship with Jesus Christ, the true and only God. As you read, I hope you see some things that make you say, "Wow, really, that could happen to a young person." Or for you to say, "Yeah, I feel that way, I can relate to that empty feeling inside of me."

I was lost, dying, hurting, and suffering and <u>no one</u> told me about God. They told me the religious things to do, but they never told me about a relationship with Jesus Christ. It wasn't until I forced my born-again friend to tell me what she meant when she said she was a born-again Christian, that I understood.

I have been praying for you long before you picked up this book. I'm praying this will go through the nations and anyone that is broken, hurting, or trying to fill a hole with anything but Jesus Christ, will come to know Him and love Him as I do.

> I knew you in your mother's womb
> before you were even born.
> Jeremiah 1:5

I was conceived in deception, lies and cheating.
But in the midst of that God had a plan and a purpose for my life.

Bridget Johnson

How it All Began

Please allow me to introduce myself. My name is Bridget Faith Dinwiddie, Durham, Smith, Johnson. Dinwiddie was my last name at birth, Durham the name I went by from the time I was two years old until 18, Smith my first married name and now Johnson, my forever married name.

I remember growing up as a child and as a young adult, I desperately wanted the hole in my heart to be filled up. I wanted to know God was truly alive and that He had a purpose for my life. Unfortunately, no one took the time to tell me. I went to a religious church that said, "Get water baptized, join the church, and live a good life." All the while, the garbage that was happening in the church was atrocious. It was a bigoted denomination along with an intolerant environment, that told me nothing about who Jesus Christ, the Son and our Savior, really is.

I lived across the street from a Pentecostal Church that knew all about religion. The rules were 'don't cut your hair, don't wear makeup, wear dresses all the time (including when you go swimming)' it was all about religion. I'm sure some people loved God in both churches and wanted to serve Him. The problem was that there was a hurting and dying nation right outside of their doors. In fact, I always thought of both churches as a social club that I wasn't allowed to join. How sad! Once someone did knock on our door to evangelize and tell us about Jesus, but when he saw a pornographic magazine on the floor he said we were too bad to get saved. Once again, a form of religion, but he was judging us based on what he saw. I was dying a slow death and no one wanted to rescue me.

I'll never forget the little goody-good Christians who

tried to get us "saved." You know, the ones with the soft white hands and white preppy shirts? These were the "perfect" Christian boys and girls who had never been abused; they grew up in the 'Beaver Cleaver' life and had no idea that I was being molested and that my mother was being raped and beaten regularly. They weren't willing to come down from their glass palaces to see what was going on.

I never want to be that way. I never want to stand before someone on Judgement Day and have them say to me, "Why didn't you tell me?" I firmly believe that it's important to live your life as a Christian and set an example without being preachy. But I also think there's a time and a place when you lay it on the line for someone.

***

I went to an altar one night after a Teen Challenge Meeting. I got down on my knees and begged God to deliver my dad from alcoholism and to see him serving God by preaching to all the drunks in the bars he had ever known. I prayed for him for deliverance for 20 years. Then one day, as clear as anything, the Holy Spirit said to me, "Your dad will get saved, but it will be a death bed experience."

While I was growing up, I didn't have a very good relationship with him. His alcoholic behavior and his abuse made it almost impossible for me to care about him. He says he loved me and I'm assuming that he did, but his behavior didn't portray much love. After I got married and my parents divorced, I moved to California. The distance between us made it that much harder. With me in California and him in Missouri, we never spoke and we certainly didn't write letters. What little relationship we had, virtually died.

If you are sold out to God and you're around people, even blood (or not blood as in my case) family who don't share the same beliefs, then you don't have a whole lot in common. I know my dad was a broken man from the day he was born, considering the life he was born into. For that I'm sorry.

But you can't play the victim card forever. He had a choice to make. He could have made the choice to find God, find inner healing and be a decent human being, but he didn't. I remember when his second biological daughter called me at work and said, "If you want to see your dad again before he dies, you better come now." I hadn't seen the man or even really talked to him for about 10 years at that point.

I couldn't bring myself to talk to him. He had always, always been drunk. I started to have flashbacks of his behavior when I had talked to him when he was drunk. Was I wrong? Maybe, but I did what I had to do to preserve some semblance of sanity.

When I got the call, I knew I couldn't take my husband because my ex-husband was sure to show up to meet the man that stole me from him. That was ridiculous because we had been divorced for 10 years before I ever met Peter. But in the small town life I lived, my ex-husband was a part of my dad's life and I suspected he would be there. I decided I needed to see Dad. When I arrived, the ex was there.

My friend, Lory, said she would make the drive with me. When I arrived, true-to-form my dad was sitting at the table with a beer in one hand and a cigarette in the other. He looked bad, but not deathly. I said to him, "I thought you were about dead?"

He said, "Nope not yet." But of course, his beer-drinking cirrhosis of the liver was getting him closer and closer to that coffin.

I sat by him and we had a little chat. If you're Baptist, you will understand this. I asked him if he knew where he was going when he passed away. He said, "Yes, that he had gotten right with his Maker and he was ready to go." For a Baptist that meant he had repented. It was about 1 or 2 years later when he went on hospice and ultimately passed away. I talked to him one more time before he went and I asked him if he was sure he knew where he was going. He said, "I told you I got right with my Maker."

I truly believe with all my heart that my dad got saved on his deathbed. He never preached to the broken, hurting people in the bars, my mother never led anyone to Christ, and yet their reward is heaven itself. They had so much to live for, so many things God wanted to do through them and for them, but they lived for what they wanted.

If I had never committed my life to the Lord, would they have made heaven? Would we all be dead and maybe in a sinner's hell? I think so. I remember one time when I was at my lowest point as a baby Christian. I told the Lord I had had enough and I just couldn't go on with Him anymore. The battle had been hard and I was spent. Then as clear as anything the Lord said to me, "If you walk away from Me, what will happen to your family? Your family will go to hell because no one is standing in the gap for them." Because I loved my family, even though we didn't have a relationship, I wanted them to make heaven their eternal home.

So I brushed off my proverbial knees and said, "Okay, God, I will live for you another day."

I love Jesus Christ with every fiber of my being, but there have been times I thought I couldn't go on. Long before I actually divorced my ex-husband, the Lord said to me in my heart one day, "Sit down I want to have a talk with you." I sat down to listen and the Lord said, "Do you want a divorce, yes or no?" I had to think long and hard about it. I didn't really feel like I wanted to get a divorce at that time. I felt like I still had some life in the marriage that I wanted to fight for, but I had to think about it first.

I finally said, "No Lord, I don't want a divorce."

Then as clear as anything, He said to my heart, "This is what would have happened if you said yes. You would have been divorced, but you also would have walked away from Me (God). But because you have to worship something and you have to bow down to some god you would have moved to San Francisco and became a Satan-worshipper." I knew beyond a shadow of doubt that would have been true. I would have interrupted my destiny. I would have walked away from everything that was good and holy so I could live the way I wanted to live.

***

I've been to the dark side of life. When I was a teenager in the 70's, there was a magazine that came out that explained about how to become a teenage witch. There were ads in the back of the magazine where you could buy potions and learn different incantations. I got into the Ouija board and I can tell you that it is driven by a demonic spirit. I also had sleep-overs and we would do séances and chant different things. We even levitated people.

I read the trashiest novels you can imagine. They were so graphic, they should have been outlawed. Today, it's raunchy books turned into movies. No Christian in his right mind should ever read or look at that garbage. It comes straight from the pits of hell. But, Christians and people that call themselves Christians are dabbling on the dark side all the time.

How could someone that says they want to serve Jesus and be all He wants them to be, end up in a bar on a Friday or Saturday night drinking beer and thinking it's funny and fun? I've lived those dark nights and that's when I was in the pit of hell and despair.

I talk about my mother, my mother's mother, their lives of sadness and despair and wrong choices. The Bible says in Jeremiah 1:5; "I knew you in your mother's womb before you were even born." I was conceived in deception, lies and cheating. But in the midst of that, God had a plan and a purpose for my life.

My self-esteem was low. An illegitimate child in that time was an automatic branding of a Scarlet A on the mother's chest. It was also a huge stigma on the kid. As the illegitimate child, I can tell you that you always look at yourself as the biggest mistake your mother ever created. In the beginning my mother said she loved me and wanted me and that my biological father loved me and maybe I was a gift to him in his old age. But even if none of that was true, God the Father loved me and yes, if I had been the only person on Earth, He would have died for me to set me free.

But I didn't know that, couldn't know that, until I found a relationship in Him. Growing up, I remember times I was severely depressed and suicidal. My heart was broken much of the time. All the people who said they loved me mistreated me in some form or another.

Because of the sexual abuse and my miserable marriage, I allowed myself to get heavy. I remember one day the Holy Spirit saying to me, "Bridget, I'm not telling you to lose weight so you can cheat on your husband. You need to do it for your health." My weight was a barrier so no one would abuse me sexually again. I've met lots of heavy women and I would have to say a lot of them have been sexually abused in some form or another. Being fat makes you feel safe so no one will abuse you anymore. Unfortunately that doesn't keep the predators away.

There was much sadness and despair in my life. But guess what? There is a happy ending. The righteousness of God has made me complete. I'm born-again, Spirit-filled and I have a purpose for being on the earth. God loves me, He died for me, He set me free of my broken heart.

I don't live on a mountain top every day of my life and float on a cloud of cotton candy. I get beaten up and bogged down, and I get aggravated and mad when my plans don't go the way I want them to.

I lost the teen years with my son that I will never get back. Poor choices were made on his dad's part, my part and yes, on his part. My son didn't speak to me for 2 ½ years and I didn't know if he was alive or dead. But I had my promise from God, *he will eat slop with the pigs and come home*.

My son and I have a good relationship now. We're both

pretty opinionated and sometimes we get aggravated at each other. He cut me out of his life again not too long ago for a few months. I've learned to find common ground to talk to him about, listen when he wants to talk and pray for him regularly. He knows what the call is on his life and one day he will do it.

My Mother

It's important to the story to talk about my mother. When you know the history and background of who my mother was, it will be a little easier to see how my story grows from her and her life.

My grandmother, was raised in a very affluent family in a small town in Missouri. They had sharecroppers or day-laborers working on their property regularly. I don't know why my grandmother wasn't attracted to one of the wealthy boys of the town, but she wasn't. She was attracted to two day-laborers. I don't know the whole story except my grandfather got into a knife fight with another man over her. The other man said, "No woman is worth dying for" and ran away. My grandmother and my grandfather got married. However, because the family disapproved of him, they disowned her.

Mother said it was so sad. It was the depression era and a lot of people were very poor and hungry, my grandparents in particular. Grandmother's family was mean to her when they went through the town with their vegetable truck selling their wares. They still insisted my grandmother pay for whatever she got. To say she chose a hard life is an understatement. Grandmother had one child who was severely deformed and died shortly after birth. In five year increments she gave birth to her oldest daughter, her only son, and my mother. I'm not quite sure why the five-year pattern, but that's what happened. It is possible grandmother had miscarriages in between but no one is alive now to tell the rest of that story.

When my mother was a child she slept in the same bed as my grandmother. When my mother was seven years old, she tried to wake her mother up. She wanted grandmother to make breakfast, but for some reason she wouldn't wake up. Grandmother had passed away in the night. Mother's sister was 17 at the time. My grandfather was still a migrant, not a very hard worker, and an alcoholic. He couldn't take care of any of the kids. The oldest had to be responsible for my uncle and my mother. Mother never really told me how things went for her brother. I know he joined the army as soon as he could. As far as I know, he ended up a beggar on the streets looking for food most of his life.

My aunt didn't want to take care of my mother and she was certainly too young to do that, but what was she supposed to do? She wouldn't send my mother to an orphanage, I guess they existed then but who knows. It was 1942 so I have no idea what was going on in that town. To help take care of my mother financially, my aunt married her first husband at 17. I don't think he was a good man but I don't remember that part.

Mother said at age 12 she had to have her adenoids removed which caused her to be almost totally deaf. So now her sister has a 12-year-old that can barely hear. Mother said school days were terrible because her sister wouldn't always give her lunch money. Mother was hungry a lot. Maybe her sister was too, but it's unclear.

For future information, if I don't know the story, I will just not fill in the blanks.

When mother was in 7th grade, probably shortly after the operation, she quit school. She was almost totally deaf and the teachers were cruel. Instead of putting her up closer to the front they put her in the back row. She wasn't learning and she was hungry, so why stay in school?

When she turned 15, she decided to go to Texas to visit her brother who was in the army. She would go back and forth between her only two living relatives. I'm sure both loved her in their own way, but they were too young to be responsible for a teenager fulltime, so they allowed her to travel back and forth between the two of them.

Her brother had a girlfriend that was only 13 years old. He was 21 years old. This young woman really wanted to get married. Probably the same reason lots of women got married in those days – army husband, secure income, he was a nice man and the pictures showed he was rather attractive. However, my uncle was a little skittish about marrying a 13-year-old girl. Somehow, it got into this girls' head that if my mother married his friend, then the uncle would marry her. She begged until my mother said yes. 15 years old and my mother married for the first time. Mother had no idea about sex or babies or the like.

After some time, she went back home to Missouri to see her sister. She was back and forth on a regular basis because she was looking for "home." Isn't that what we all do – look for home? Mother miscarried a baby on one of those back and forth trips. I know I have an older brother or sister in heaven. I hope they greeted my mother when she arrived.

Eventually my mother divorced her husband and moved back to Missouri where her sister lived. During that time my mother married for the second time. I don't know much about their lives other than they were married for seven years. She tried to have a baby with him but it didn't work out.

Mother had separated from her second husband, hadn't divorced him yet, and was working when she was "introduced" to my biological father. I use the term "introduced" loosely, because money changed hands if you know what I mean? My mother's sister was dating an older, successful and married business man at the time. Apparently when he came to see my aunt, he brought his "friend" to meet her sister. He thought my mother was a pretty young thing. He was much older – about 30 years is what I think mother told me. He wined and dined her. He took her to nice restaurants where she got to wear a cocktail dress. He was

Rags to Righteousness

very generous with her and with the people in the restaurants. If you want to imagine how nice the restaurant was – just think of an old movie where they had cigarette girls walking around and everyone is dressed to the nines.

It was the 50's – there wasn't an actual war going on at that time, but it was the time of worrying about war – so I'm sure the attitude of the day was "let's party hearty because tomorrow we may die." There was one major problem between them. Not only was my mother married and separated, but my biological father was married and living with his wife. I'm not sure what number mistress she was.

Mother said after a couple of times being with my bio father, she became pregnant. I asked her if she really knew who my biological father was. She said yes, of course, she knew who he was. I do look a lot like him so it's pretty evident, even without a DNA test, who I belong to.

She moved to St. Louis to be closer to my biological father. She had a job at a drug store where she made milk shakes. She didn't know she was pregnant with me because she was still having her period.

From the beginning of my conception, the enemy tried many, many times to take my life. Before mother knew she was pregnant with me, she had taken some hallucinogenic drug that made her think she could fly. She started to jump out of her second story apartment when my biological father showed up and stopped her.

The second time the enemy tried to kill me was in her fourth month of pregnancy. Mother didn't know she was pregnant with me yet. She went to the doctor but the pregnancy tests kept coming back negative. There was not much evidence that she was pregnant, so what was wrong with her? Finally, the doctor decided to do an X-ray of her abdomen. They told her she had a tumor the size of a grapefruit and they needed to take it out immediately. Once they opened her up – lo and behold there I was. Mother said when they told her she was pregnant she thought they were lying and she really had a tumor.

After I was successfully born, mother said I was in my bassinet and "something" (now, of course, we know it was God) told her to check my bassinet – she looked under the mattress and there was a deadly black widow spider.

Mother told me, "As a baby/toddler, I was a much loved and a wanted child." I found a picture of me as a toddler about 18 months old and I'm in a satin dress. A satin dress on a toddler could only come from someone wealthy.

When I turned 33, I had a severe identity crisis. I called my mother crying and asked her if my biological father loved me or was merely a sperm donor. She told me the story of what happened one day when he came to see me. He always wore a mustache. But for some reason I didn't like it that day. He tried to pick me up out of my walker and hold me. However, I protested and wouldn't let him touch me. He promptly walked into the bathroom and shaved. He told my mother that he hadn't shaved that mustache off for anyone in over 30 years. I was happy to know that I was wanted.

Mother was still trying to find "home" and love in all the wrong places. She decided to move out of the city where my biological father lived and moved back to the small town where her sister was. After the move, my biological father and mother continued to "date." My biological father wanted to marry my mother, but she didn't love him and didn't want him to lose everything. In those days all of his wealth and life would have been destroyed in a nasty divorce. Even though his wife was a cheater as well, she would look like the victim. So mother refused to marry him, but continued to date him and another man.

Apparently during that time frame, my biological father tried to "buy" me from my mother's sister. He told her he would buy her a brand new car if she would get mother to give me up.

My mother became pregnant again. There was a huge dispute over who that child actually belonged to. She said she wasn't having sex with the second man, but who knows! That child caused a huge rift between my bio father and mother.

They eventually broke up, and he told her he wasn't going to send her any more money. She told him she didn't want his money anyway. That was completely foolish of her. She lived such a hard life, two illegitimate children, no place to live, and no education to help her make enough money to support all of us.

Apparently my biological father kept track of me through my aunt. I remember vividly when I was about six years old, I was hanging out with my aunt at the local gas station. My aunt lived in a house behind a gas station on a busy road. I didn't know it at the time, but my aunt was having an affair with the gas station owner so she was there quite often.

This particular day she took me with her to the gas station. I didn't know why. However, a nice looking businessman in a suit in a nice new car drove up. He came into the station where I was and picked me up and put me on the counter so we could talk eye-ball to eye-ball. He asked me if I knew who he was. I said "No, I have no idea." He told me he was my father. I said, "No you're not, my dad is off drunk somewhere, as usual."

I looked at my aunt and she said, "Yes, this is your father."

I didn't know what to think. He asked me if I would like to come and live with him. This was about 1965. He said I would have my own room, a canopy bed and my own radio. Hot dog, my own radio! At the time I was sleeping on a sleeper sofa. We didn't really have a home to live in, it was just one room from what I can remember. We didn't have much food and certainly didn't have a radio for any of us.

I responded, "Let me go ask my mom if I can go live with you." I went and told my mother who was at the station and could I go live with him. She left me at home and ran over to the station and cussed him out. She told him to never come near us again. I know beyond a shadow of a doubt my aunt would have loved to have had the money he was offering for me, but mother said she wasn't interested in selling her kids.

I will never forget that day until the day I die. I couldn't understand why she wouldn't let me go with him. I thought my life would be so glamorous and wonderful. When I was feeling sorry for myself because of the conditions we were living under, I asked her why didn't she just give me up to my bio dad. I don't recall her answer.

I asked my mother again when I was 17 why she didn't let me go live with my bio father and his family. She told me she was afraid my life would have been much worse than the conditions we were living. I would have had my bio father with his money, but she was unsure if his wife would accept me. Would she have abused me? How would he introduce me? I was a product of his mid-life crisis. So who knows what really could have happened to me.

My Early Days

Welfare virtually didn't exist in those days. My mother had little income. She was working at a bar and her paycheck went to pay for a babysitter, and a roof over our heads. She was really having a hard time trying to survive.

She met the man I call my "dad." She married him out of desperation to help support us when I was about two years old and my brother was a baby.

After she met and married my dad, he became our "father." I must use that term very loosely, because my birth certificate name was my mother's married name. However, because mother didn't want to advertise the fact that her kids weren't legally or biologically connected to my dad she gave us our dad's last name. It's interesting how different the world is now. I got my social security card under that name, but had to get my driver's license under my birth name. Because that name wasn't a very reputable name in the town I lived in, I was embarrassed to show anyone my driver's license. Can you imagine being 16, just getting your driver's license and not being able to show your friends because your last name didn't match?

During my growing up years, I hid what my last name was and how I was conceived. When I met new friends and we talked about our backgrounds and who we were, I always lied and pretended my stepdad was my biological dad. I couldn't admit to anyone that I was illegitimate. I was terribly embarrassed and I was fearful that someone would find out what my last name was, and who my actual birth father was.

Unfortunately, "my dad" was a very abusive alcoholic. The horrors that I witnessed! He was a sick, tormented man.

Bridget Johnson

He lived the only way he knew, which was alcohol and abusing my mother. My mother tried to run away from him many times, but she would always come back and she couldn't get away. Domestic violence shelters didn't exist and you were basically a property of your husband.

My mother would be savagely beaten. She or I, if I could get to a phone, would call the police. The police would see her bloody face. She would tell them what happened and they did nothing. They were drinking buddies with my dad.

As I write this, I'm sick about the memories. Those were devastating times. At one point, my mother got pregnant with my youngest sister. We were living way out in the country, my mother couldn't drive and couldn't work. In those days my mother's father lived with us. My dad would leave us for days and days out in the country. After my sister was born we basically lived on oatmeal. We didn't have milk for the baby so my mother would walk to the neighbors and beg for milk. I can't remember, but I'm assuming since she's alive today someone gave my mother milk for her. Eventually she talked my dad into moving us back into town. Probably so she could work to help provide for us.

I remember one time very vividly. I had to be younger than five. My mother had fixed fried chicken for dinner. Grandpa wanted another piece of chicken. My mom told him no because we hadn't eaten yet. She was trying to keep her 3 kids fed. We lived on bread and gravy just so we could exist. On the day my grandfather passed away – he told my mom as he was leaving to go to the bar, to take his social security check and "buy those kids some apples." Fruit was a luxury for us. Whenever we got any kind of fruit, we felt rich. Grandpa died that day and so did a lot of my mother's emotional and financial support.

Times got worse. We lived in a basement apartment and shared a bathroom with our neighbor. My sister was about two, when grandpa passed away. She heard someone in the bathroom and thought it was grandpa. She kept calling out to papa. That day that wonderful man, our neighbor, became our adopted grandfather. He was a very kind and good man. He was single and definitely old enough to be our grandfather. We got to go to his apartment, spend the night when mother and daddy went out drinking and he was the one thing basically normal in our lives.

We eventually moved out of that basement apartment, but papa stayed in our lives as much as possible. My dad was jealous of papa because we loved him and he had the money and time to spend with us. He took us fishing and he would provide treats for us.

***

When it was time for me to go to kindergarten, I didn't get to go. My mother had no money to buy me clothes for school. Somehow she came up with money to get me some school clothes for me to go to first grade. Mother was working as a maid at a hotel so I'm guessing that's where the money came from.

People today act like they can't go to work if it rains. We lived in Missouri and it was cold and the snow would get deep. She walked to work in that kind of weather. She walked to and from that hotel for years and years. It had to be a minimum of 5 miles one way. She tried so hard. But, because of the mental and verbal abuse and everything else you can imagine being thrown at her, she was always sick. I remember walking home from school and thinking if mother had on her makeup today it would be a good day. More times than not she didn't have her makeup on, and she would be stretched out on the couch sick. She would want us to brush her hair, or wash her face, something to comfort her.

I couldn't go outside to play much because I had to clean the house or cook dinner.

My childhood was very hard. The enemy of our souls, the devil, has tried since conception to kill me. As I mentioned before, the doctor thought I was a tumor and then the spider in the bassinet incident, but it didn't stop there. When I was a baby I couldn't eat and keep food down. For six years, my mother, took me to a string of doctors to find out why I was thin and sickly. The doctor told my mom that I was born with damaged tonsils. They literally dripped poison into my system and that's why I couldn't eat. He told her I needed surgery but she didn't want to put me through that. I was so young. However, I heard the doctor tell my mom without the surgery I would die. I remember asking my mother if I was going to die.

Within a few days I was in the hospital getting my tonsils out and living on ice cream and gelatin. My dad brought me roses to the hospital. It was so sweet of him.

Grandma's House

I loved to go to my grandma's house. She lived about 1 to 2 hours away from where we lived. As far as I was concerned, I didn't get to go to grandma's house often enough. Grandma's mother was alive as well so we had two grandmothers' alive to go and visit.

However, at grandma's house it was a bit of a dangerous place for me. Two uncles molested me. My parents both went to their graves not knowing that I had been sexually abused. One of them didn't abuse me for very long. I was so young I barely remember the inappropriate touch. However, the second one – that abuse went on for some time. I was 11 and he was 13 or 14. My brother, sister and I used to sleep in the same bed with my abuser. I had no idea what was happening was so wrong, plus there was no one to tell because no one would have believed me. As I got older, someone suspected something because he wasn't allowed to be around me anymore.

However, I always wanted to go to grandma's house in spite of the abuse because there was still a sense of family there. My dad had 6 brothers. Grandma raised 7 boys, can you just imagine? Grandpa was also an alcoholic abuser. The fruit doesn't fall far from the tree. I don't think all the boys abused their wives – some of the wives wouldn't have put up with it – the other more broken boys – like my dad – were the more abusive ones.

I had a cousin that was several years older and I absolutely loved hanging out with her at grandma's house. She would take me with her everywhere she went. I was like her live doll. One day, when I was about six, we went to the city pool. She told me not to walk too close to the pool. I did and water splashed and I slipped and fell. I remember hitting bottom and I blacked out. She saved me that day. To this day I'm terrified of water. I would love to go on a cruise with my husband, however, the thought of being on water is more than I can bear.

At grandma's house, my mom and dad behaved – no abuse. At grandma's house we always, always had enough food. At grandma's house, except for those two uncles, I felt relatively safe in my bubble of a family.

Then we would leave grandma's house and return to our nightmare at home.

Growing Up Years

My growing-up years was more of the same. Either my dad was beating my mother, or he was off on an alcoholic tangent and he wasn't home. My idea of sex was so trashed that except by the grace of God I wouldn't have had a healthy sex life. My parents would take us to the drive-in theater. However, we didn't go see family movies. We went to raunchy, vile, sexual movies. The movies were so vile they should have been rated X and that's in the 60's. I was the only one that stayed awake and watched the pornography. Then I would wake mom and dad up and say, "Time to go home, the movies are over."

Saturday was allowance day. However, in order to get our allowance, we had to ride with daddy to the bar. We were allowed to go in the bar to get a soda early in the day. When it got to be dusk outside we could no longer go in there. We would get our $1.00 a week allowance and be set free to run around "up-town" to spend our money. Wow! You could spend that $1.00 a hundred different ways. Today, if kids don't get $10, they can't do anything, not even get into the movies.

We would come back after spending our money. Daddy was pretty drunk by then and he would let us leave. We would walk home at that point and get away from the darkness. I hated going into that bar. There was a lady there in stretch white shorts – you know the ones that have a seam down the front – and pantyhose. She would be hung over from the night before, trying to sober up to get drunk again when the sun went down. I remember in my later years when I committed my life to Christ I just knew my dad would get saved and he would tell her about the Lord and she would get saved. I heard later she died – beaten up by some boyfriend that took her out – got drunk and then murdered her.

When I was 14, I told my dad I wasn't going to that bar anymore. I couldn't stand the darkness, the drunk people and the sadness. He told me I was going to be cut off from my allowance, I didn't care. I said I would make my own money. I didn't return to that bar until I was 18 or 19 years old and I had started drinking and carrying on myself.

As he got older dad became a mechanic for a heavy construction equipment company. He made really good money when he worked. The problem was he worked seasonal and he didn't know how to make the money stretch. He would rather hang out at the bar looking like a big shot spending money on booze or on other women.

Our "Church" Life

I use this phrase quite loosely because my growing up life was far from any kind of spiritual awakening or training.

My parents were both Southern Baptist in name only. When we were made to go to church that's the kind we went to. My aunt made us go with her. There wasn't much point because I fell asleep most of the time during the service. Sunday school wasn't too bad, but I would have rather slept in on Sunday than go to church.

We did have one other person that took us to church. Her name was Mrs. Smith, but we called her old lady Mrs. Smith. She usually tried to get us to go Sunday night or Wednesday night. Sometimes we would want to go, but lots of times, the rotten kids we were, we would hide behind our mother and make her tell old lady Mrs. Smith we didn't want to go. Bless her heart she was trying to save the heathen kids.

One summer we went to vacation bible school. I really did try to pay attention and actually learn something. I think from a young age I had a call on my life and I wanted to serve God. But how could I? I had seen a commercial that said, "Is God dead?" I'll never forget that guy walking on the beach and saying that. I started wondering if God was dead. It was the 70's. The Jesus movement hit, but it was more of a hippie thing to me.

I learned some things in VBS and I did earn some awards. I remember my dad gave me a locket-like necklace when I graduated that week from VBS. It was a picture of Jesus no less. Because my dad actually took an interest in me, I loved it. I carried that thing around for years. One time

I got mad at him and threw it away.

In the Baptist Church, if you didn't belong to the church, you couldn't take communion. The only way you could join the church was to be baptized. I was really intrigued by communion, every time it went by I wanted one of those crackers and some of that juice. One day I told my aunt that I wanted some. She said I needed to join the church first. I said, "Okay, how do I do that?"

Well true to a Southern Baptist Church, that day they had their usual altar call asking people to come forward who wanted to join the church. The song everyone was singing was "Just as I Am." I went up to the altar and shook hands with the pastor. He said, "Do you want to join the church and get baptized?"

I said, "Yes I did." I was crying so hard, I had no idea why. I know now it was the conviction of the Holy Spirit. I will remember that day forever. I was 9 years old at the time.

Several days later my water baptism was scheduled. I was told if you fight the pastor when you go under the water you have a devil inside you. I was so afraid to get in that water, I just knew I had a devil and it was going to get loose.

I didn't fight, I got baptized and I was fine. However, an older lady in the congregation did try to get baptized, but she got scared and she did fight the pastor. That poor woman was so humiliated. She just knew she had a devil. I never knew what became of her. So sad how silly church doctrine and made up stuff can be in the church.

I tried to live for God after that. I only really knew one prayer and that was the lay me down to sleep one. But because the church we went to preached hell fire and damnation every service, I knew I was going to die in the night and go to hell. So just about every night of my life from the time I was 9 years old until I actually got saved I said, "Lord forgive me of my sins and if I die tonight, please let me go to heaven." Every day I got up and lived the same way I did before. I didn't know how to change, didn't know how to allow God to change me.

I continued to go to that church until I was 13. Remember, my dad was an alcoholic, my mother was physically and emotionally sick all the time. So when we went to church we went with my aunt. However, my aunt moved away and we started walking to church, just the 3 of us, my brother, sister and me.

One day when we were in Sunday school I asked the teacher if Jesus was married. I kid you not she said, "We don't know those things, they're not in the Bible." Then I asked her if he had kids, same answer. Really, that poor Sunday school teacher didn't even know who Jesus was. We never heard anything about the Holy Spirit. We believed in the Trinity, but I have no idea who we thought the Holy Spirit was.

The last straw was when we were walking home from church and the matriarch of the church's kids starting making fun of us. Calling us trashy names, poor people, you name it. These were supposed to be the people that love you and care for you no matter what. I went home and told my mother, "You can beat me, but I will never go to that church again." In fact, I didn't go there again for almost 30 years. It was after my mother died and I was in town and the Lord told me to go to that church. I said, "No way, I'm not doing it." But, I ended up going anyway. That pastor was still teaching hell fire and brimstone to the same congregation 30 years later. I saw that Sunday school teacher and I wanted to tell her so bad Jesus wasn't married and didn't have kids. I didn't. I heard not too long after that she died. I'm glad I wasn't mean and rude at the end of her life.

That was the end of my "spiritual journey," or so I thought. I remember being in my bunk-bed, top bunk no less, and the Holy Spirit said to me, "I want you to serve me."

I can't, I don't even know who you are, maybe you're dead. For years He dealt with me until I got to the point that I said, "If you ever show Yourself real to me, I'll serve You all the days of my life." He did just that several years later.

During the time of my wild teenage years, I tried to find God again. I had a Catholic friend and she invited me to go to church with her. The symbolism of it was awesome. I just loved that church and everything about it.

The symbolism and the ritual of it really drew me. I decided that I wanted to become a nun. If I didn't get married by the time I was 25, I was going to commit myself to the church and go on the mission field. The jungles of Brazil were my chosen place.

I signed up for mail-order catechism classes and got excellent grades on everything. I knew how to pray to Mary, I was getting ready for my first communion, the whole bit. Problem, my family wasn't Catholic and I was too old to try and find god-parents. I would need to be accepted in the Catholic Church as an adult but I needed a sponsor. That summer I even wanted to go to nun novice school. My parents refused to let me go. I had to work instead of seeking God in a monastery.

Well, the priest tried to find me a sponsor and no one wanted me. What?! The one true church, my one chance to get into heaven through the Catholic Church, and I was told no. How could that happen? No one wanted to sponsor a poor girl from the wrong side of the tracks. In my town you were either Catholic or Protestant and the Catholics had the corner on being on the wealthy side of town.

I couldn't find God in the Baptist Church and not in the Catholic Church. I was pretty crushed by that. I couldn't believe the teaching of the Catholic Church that said it was the "one" true church and the only way to heaven. However, the people that were on their way to heaven had no interest in helping me get there.

I was back to nowhere. I was lonely and empty inside and full of despair.

Forced to Grow Up Too Fast

Up until I was 12 years old, my mother managed to buy the three of us our school clothes. She would put our clothes on lay-a-way at a dime store. Five outfits, new shoes, five new sets of underclothes, and a new coat every other year. I don't know how she did that with her income but she managed.

Right before school was out when I was going to be 12, my mother told me she couldn't buy my school clothes anymore and I needed to get a job. Yes, it's good for kids to learn how to work, but to the point that you have to support yourself and buy your own school clothes is not the way to live. I baby-sat that summer and made enough money to buy my own clothes. I got them at the end-of-summer sidewalk sales. I thought I had the cutest clothes until I got to school to find out they were already outdated. Of course they were, *it was the end-of-summer clearance*. We didn't know how to buy classic pieces that you mix and match. It was the 70's, hip hugger pants and body suits were the norm. I wanted toe socks and platform shoes along with my huge bell bottom pants.

My teen years were pretty much the same as my elementary years except emotionally things were harder for me. I was always looking for love in all the wrong places. I had a God-size hole in my heart that I was trying to fill with drugs and eventually sex and alcohol.

A year or so before I started dating, my mother and I had a talk about my future. My mother promised me a set of white Samsonite luggage as a wedding gift if I made it to my wedding day as a virgin. Back in 1975 that was a huge deal. The sexual revolution hadn't hit our small town in Missouri so it was every young girl's plan to be a virgin on their wedding night.

I wasn't supposed to start dating until I was 16. However, when I was 15 my best friend got an invitation to a dance at the Military Academy. It was an all-male school and the families were pretty wealthy. They had to be, to be able to support the tuition. We went to the dance and had a really good time.

After the dance, my best friend met someone and he was "kind of her boyfriend." It was harder in those days with the boys being in Military School to see them very much. But I was told her boyfriend had a friend who had just arrived at the school. Did I want to meet him? Of course, I did! I desperately wanted a boyfriend and I wanted to meet him. I walked as fast as I could to her house, ran into the bathroom to "freshen up" and then I set my eyes on him. For me it was truly love at first sight. Not infatuation, in fact later after he left the school, my mother admitted knowing that I truly loved him and she had wished she had allowed me to marry him.

We went on some dates, but remember, I was a naïve virginal little girl and this boy had "lived." I say I was virginal because I was never raped and never had intercourse with my abusers. He had already had sex, he had been in and out of jail and was a pretty heavy drinker and drug user. We dated, if you can call it that, from October until he left for Christmas break. When he came back from Christmas break, everything was different. He didn't want to be around me and I was devastated. He was the first boy I ever kissed and made out with. He had stolen my heart and we had talked about our future together.

By the time he left the school in April, I was hysterical. I will never forget what my best friend told me the day she came to school and told me he had left. He said to tell you, "I love you too much to take you to the place where I'm going." We didn't have a phone so Chris couldn't call me and tell me goodbye himself.

I was suicidal over the thought that he was gone. On my bad days – I would listen to Donny Osmond sing "…and they called it Puppy Love" and on a really bad day I would listen to some dark song from Alice Cooper. Side note – when I committed my life to Jesus Christ on January 4, 1981 – I asked the Lord for two things: One, to see Chris again and tell him about Jesus and give him a chance to be saved before he died and two, to have a baby. God gave me both of those *things*.

Even to a crushed 15-year-old girl, life goes on. I was still looking for love in all the wrong places. I wasn't getting it at home, I wasn't getting it from the boys at school and the guys I met at the Military Academy were after that "one" thing. I wasn't a virgin at that point, but I still didn't want to be "easy."

I had an older relative in my mid-teen years that I became very close to. She was the big sister I never had and I liked to hang out with her. She was going through some really bad times and she took me right along with her. She met a guy at a carnival; turns out he was on parole for something. So we decided since she had a boyfriend, I needed a boyfriend. Our town was a town of 10,000 so we decided to go ride around and find me a boyfriend. We literally picked up some strange guy, early 20's, sitting in front of the pool hall. He didn't have anything better to do. We went back to his house that night, smoked pot, drank and did some things I'm very ashamed of. Guess what? He was on parole as well.

The more we hung out, the more concerned everyone was about the guys being on parole. I was still a naïve 16-year-old girl trying to feel love. Because of that, I was pretty much willing to do whatever they wanted to do. When the guys decided they didn't want to go back to prison they made a plan for us to pack up and leave. Because they were on parole and the likelihood of them going back to prison was very high, we needed to get out of town quickly. They were still doing the things they went to prison for, growing/smoking pot and dealing drugs. The funny thing, is what in the world did we think changing zip codes would do? They had no education, no desire to do better and make something of their lives. If they did, they could have done it there as easily as anywhere else.

Everyone got the brilliant idea that we would pack up and move somewhere else and get a fresh start. I had no idea that what we were doing would land the guys back in prison or that my cousin could go to jail for taking a minor across state lines. She had a baby girl and we had no money. It was a perfect recipe for bad things to happen. I was miserable at home and the cousin – well what did she have to lose? We loaded up in her car and headed for California. Yup, sure did – the 4 of us were on the run from the law and everything that I thought was bad at home couldn't be any worse on the run.

It was tons worse! I was pimped out for a night. The idea was for me to get a "date" and while we were walking to wherever to do the deal, the boys would jump him and roll him for his money. Isn't that pleasant? However, the plan went wrong. They lost track of me. I ended up with this horrible stranger telling me about how life could be so good if I just came to live with him and let him take care of me. How much money I could make blah, blah…. Fortunately for me, my cousin really did care about me and she managed to find me and get me out of there.

During this nightmare, I thought I was pregnant, we were hungry, and we barely had any place to sleep. The boys were on parole, I was barely 16 and the cousin has a little 2-year-old she was trying to take care of. If not for the grace of God…the police stopped the car; I think my cousin's boyfriend ran a red light or something. When the police started investigating, they found out the guys were on parole and I was a runaway. Amber Alert's didn't exist in those days, but they still had a way of getting word out to all the right police stations to let them know I was a runaway.

I was immediately arrested and I spent a night in the county jail – I'll never forget the sound of those clanging jail cell doors.

I was transferred to a juvenile detention center. It was absolutely horrid. I couldn't eat, too scared to eat after they told me how I should wear my socks and be careful of someone attacking and/or raping me. I just wanted to go home. However, when I talked to my mother on the phone she told me I could stay in California and rot. She had had enough of me. My dad managed to come up with the money to fly me home.

When I got home I had a ring of hickey's around my neck, but I refused to admit I had been having sex. They wanted me to testify against the guy for statutory rape, but I refused. As far as I was concerned, I had gotten the guy into bed, it wasn't his fault I was only 16. Besides, I was afraid of retaliation against me by his relatives.

I had to go back to school, had to try to survive the stigma, the loss of my boyfriend, and I lost contact with my cousin. During that time, I got a very bad infection. I'll spare you the gory details but when I went to the doctor for treatment he said it was the worst case of infection he had ever seen especially in a 16-year-old girl's body. He asked me if I was on birth control. Of course I wasn't. My parents would kill me for using birth control. Fortunately, I never got pregnant.

I will divert from my story for just a moment here. I'm going to climb up on my soapbox and say this. I was 16 years old and had a horrid infection. But I was able to go to the doctor on my own and get treatment. My mother never knew how bad things were, she just paid the bills. Today young girls can get birth control and abortions without their parent's knowledge or consent. Looking back I wonder how did my mother not know or suspect what was happening?

Okay, Off the Soapbox Now

After I was home and my boyfriend was in jail, I started writing him letters. I thought I was so clever I got a P.O. box. Once again our town is so small the post master asked my dad why I had a P.O. Box and was getting letters from the town where the county jail was. My dad came home that night and started screaming at my mom about my behavior. He told her I was writing to a convict, blah, blah. He started to smack her around when I came out of my bedroom and screamed at him. It was my fault, not hers, and if he wanted to take it out on someone he needed to take it out on me. I also told him to go to hell, get out of our house, no one wanted him there. My brother came barreling out of his room about that time and my dad told him he would beat the hell out of him, he better get out of his way.

The next day my dad packed his bags and decided to live on the road while he worked. When I turned 18 years old, they divorced. After I had cussed out my dad, my behavior really got bad. With dad out of the house and my mother either physically or mentally sick, I was totally out of control. She tried to give me a curfew, she tried to make me behave, but I was so broken inside I didn't know how to stop.

I continued to try to fill that God- sized hole in my heart. Drinking, having sex with God only knows who, taking chances on getting pregnant; doing drugs and ending up in hotel room with a man I didn't know after I had had too much booze and drugs. I was spiraling out of control. I wanted the pain inside of my heart to stop hurting, I wanted to pick myself up by my bootstraps, but I didn't know how and when I could do it.

At this point, I had already lost my virginity, ran away with two convicts on parole, been in jail, been in a Juvenile detention center, had a horrible venereal disease, and I wasn't even 18 years old.

At 17, I was working at the store where my mother used to buy our school clothes and my supervisor asked if I wanted to go dancing with her and her boyfriend. I said I didn't have a date. The guys I was dating were pretty messed up and I didn't allow them to go out in public with me. She said, "No problem" and pulls out a fist full of pictures of guys. They were all guys she had dated. She said, "Pick one and I'll call and see if he's free to go out tonight."

I picked one, and she called him. He showed up at the store, she asked him if he wanted to go dancing with us – he said yes. I thought he was cute and said okay. They came to pick me up at my house and I was horrified. It's 1977 and he's wearing polyester high water pants, white socks, loafers and a white shirt. To him, he was dressed up. To me, he was nerdy. I was used to the guys with the long hair, jeans, boots and a cool shirt. I told my dad – please don't make me go with him. My dad said, "He's finally a nice looking kid, go on and go with him."

Bless his heart. The day before he had gotten all of his teeth pulled. So here I am 17 years old, with a guy in a white shirt, high water polyester pants and no teeth. Boy howdy! When he walked me to the door to kiss me goodnight I wasn't having it. I couldn't get in the house fast enough. The next day my mom and I were talking about the date and the "kiss." I told her there was no way in this world I was kissing him.

He continued to chase me down and try to get me to date him. He would show up at my work after my shift was over and offer me a ride home. I didn't live far from home, I usually walked home. But it was dark and scary, so I accepted the rides.

Eventually we officially started dating. After a couple weeks he brought me home from a motorcycle ride. We were, like teenagers, talking on the phone. He said to me, so when are we getting married?

"We're not."

"Yes we are"

"We can't because you haven't said that word."

"What word?"

"That I love you word."

He said, "Okay, I love you when do you want to get married?" We went and bought my diamond dust engagement ring and announced we were getting married.

We told everyone but my dad. My dad wasn't happy when he found out because he wanted me to go to college. The problem was, he had told me all through high school he would pay my way through college, I just needed to do what I needed to do to get in. My mother said he was a liar and he was never going to pay for school. She said I would end up in a strange city with a big college bill and no way to take care of myself. My mother used a lie and a fear factor to keep me from going to college.

When I told my fiancé' that I wanted to go to college he said, "If you go, we'll break up." I should have said then we'll break up, but once again fear was a big deterrent.

We got married August 14, 1977. He was a decent guy but he had his own issues. He was very selfish, no motivation and literally wanted to live a blue collar life. If I had been older or more mature, I would have seen my life played out with his parents. They literally got up to go to work, came home, ate dinner, watched TV, went to bed and started over again, Monday through Friday. Friday night and Saturday night they drank and a lot of times they went dancing. Sunday, if they weren't too hung over, they went to church. None of us were Christians. It was just the "thing" to do.

The one thing I did know was this – if I didn't get away from my alcoholic abusive dad and my sick mother, I was going to repeat history by becoming like them. I saw myself one day in the very near future meeting some guy in a bar. I would probably meet an alcoholic, I might have been one by then myself, and he would more than likely be an abuser. I would marry him, have kids I couldn't take care of, divorce him and move on to the next guy. That was my family pattern. I knew I didn't want that, but I didn't realize there was so much more to life than the blue collar life he wanted to live.

When we got married, I truly wish I had been a better human being. Getting married was my escape. Like I said because of my wild behavior, my mother kept telling me when you're 18 you're out of this house. You can't live here any longer. I was freaked out. It was March and in July I would be 18, where was I going to go? How was I going to take care of myself? I had no idea how to balance a check book, pay rent, have utilities turned on, nothing. I knew nothing! So when I started dating my "blind date" and he told me he wanted to get married after two weeks of dating I said "Sure, why not?" I have to say, when I got married I truly intended to stay married. My family was a divorce statistic of its own. My mother was on husband #3, my dad wife #2, and everyone else in the family had been divorced at least once. I wanted to get married, have a family and live happily ever after. But at 18 can you really know how long forever is?

Who wouldn't jump on the chance to marry a decent guy? His family had been married forever. His brothers and sisters were married or marrying age and I liked them and I liked feeling like an adult. I remember on my wedding day coming out of the basement of the church, and my dad saying "Are you sure you want to do this?"

No, I wasn't sure. I wanted to go home to my own bed. But I didn't want to embarrass my future husband, myself and where was I supposed to go? It would have been time to enroll in college but I didn't think I had any money.

Isn't the lack of communication lovely? I didn't tell my dad I was getting married until it was too late. Because I didn't talk to him, he couldn't talk to me about the money he had already saved for me. I couldn't tell my mother "Please don't make me move out" because she had already made it pretty clear she didn't really like me.

So I told my dad yes, I was sure. Sad day I have to say. We had no money to go anywhere. We had rented a duplex apartment where we had to share the bathroom with the nosey neighbor that would come through to our side of the house to see what we were doing. We had a little party at our apartment. A guy I kind of had a crush on – two years or so younger than me said to me "So what are you going to do tonight? You want to go out and party?"

Now in my mind I had been released from a curfew and I was an adult and could make my own choices. Fortunately, I had a little common sense because my answer was "I guess I better stay with my husband since I did just get married." Not what I wanted to do at all. I wanted to go out and party and get drunk and probably have sex with this guy.

Times were tough. He didn't know how to be a good husband; I certainly didn't know how to be a wife. I remember one night I was so proud of myself I made beef stroganoff for dinner. This is almost 40 years ago and I remember it like it was yesterday. I made the stroganoff, had the candles lit for a nice candle light dinner and he says to me, "What's that slop? I'm not eating it!"

"What's that slop? That slop was supposed to be a romantic dinner."

He grew up blue collar and wanted to stay that way. I grew up blue collar, but that was not my heritage. Remember my bio father was wealthy. I wanted that lovely white collar life. I thought I would put him through college and then he would put me through college. We would eventually live this lovely white collar life. Umm, not so much. He had no interest, no matter how much I begged, pleaded, conned, or whatever wifely tools I could use would make him go to college.

During those days we fought physically. I tried everything I could do to force him to divorce me. I thought, surely if I make his life miserable enough he'll divorce me. Remember I wasn't ever going to be divorced, not by my hand, but if he did it I was the victim.

By the way, about a year after we got married we were at Grandma's house and my Aunt Dot said to me, "We sure had a good time on your money."

I said, "What money?"

She said "Your college money. Your dad had one year of school money saved and was working on the second year when you decided you were going to get married."

I asked her why didn't he tell me or give it to me? She said it was his money to do what he wanted with it so we got drunk on it. When I told my mom her usual answer was, "Well, I didn't know." Oh my gosh, I was so mad at her I could have slapped her face. I got married because I thought I had no choice and she only said, "Well, I didn't know."

Eventually we moved to a town 40 miles away from our hometown. There was no reason other than we were playing grown up and wanted to live closer to his sister and brother-in-law. We worked in a factory grave yard shift no less. We would get off early on Saturday morning, go to breakfast with 8 other people, 2 married couples, a couple having an affair at work, and two singles. We would make plans to go out on Saturday night and drink as much hard liquor as we could consume.

I had a nice little body and knew it. So when we would go drinking and dancing I would torment those guys. There were two in particular, a married a guy and the single one not interested in the other single woman. I would gyrate and rub around on them while we were dancing. Then I would dance in a way that I think would cause a harlot to blush. All the time knowing that never in a million years would I allow one of them to touch me. That only lasted about a year. The group finally went their separate ways.

One day in 1979 my husband's brother, my brother, a friend and my husband came to our apartment and said they were all going into the military. Apparently they had all been to the military recruiting offices. My brother was going in the Navy but the other 3 into the Marine Corp. They were single, of course, and were ready to ship off to boot camp. I told my husband, "There's no way you can leave me now." I wanted to live closer to my family, possibly with my mother, and I needed to make an emotional change in my mind and life to have him gone for 3 months. I needed time to plan for him to be gone several weeks and then we would be moving somewhere. He eventually went to California for his basic training and that's where we stayed for the next 17 years.

He saw the wisdom of it and waited until January, 1980 to leave for boot camp. With complete sarcasm, once again, my mother really came through for me. She found me a "room" above the bar where I had hung out as a kid. The "room" was an old converted office building. I had a small stove. The oven didn't work, you had to prop it closed with a stick, a full-size fridge, table & chairs, chest of drawers, a curtained thing for my closet, a twin bed and two night stands. My kitchen sink was a bathroom sink so you could barely wash dishes in it. I had to go down the hall to the bathroom. Because my mother was worried about where I was living, she made sure I had a telephone. Telephones in those days were not necessarily a household item. I managed to get all of my husband's and my worldly goods into that place. I paid $25.00 a week all utilities included. He-haw!!! My mother was worried about me walking down the hall to the bathroom so she also bought me a heavy bathrobe.

I couldn't park my car in front of my apartment, no parking on the street overnight. So I would have to park my car and walk from the parking lot and back to my sleazy apartment all before dark. Good thing the place I worked was literally up the street from my apartment so it was no big deal where I parked my car.

I hated that apartment and many nights I was too scared to sleep. I remember one night someone coming home drunk, hit my door and tried to get in. My heart beat out of my chest. He finally figured out it wasn't his room and went on down the hall. I would get up early in the morning, peek down the hall to see if anyone was around, run to the bathroom, try to go without stepping in some drunk guy's pee, shower and run back to my room before the drunks woke up.

I wrote my husband every day. I felt bad for him being at boot camp and I really wanted to be a good wife. I bought fruity smelling paper and I literally wrote to him 2 times a day. Finally, when he called me one time he told me to stop writing. He had gotten in so much trouble with all the letters and perfume he didn't want them. His CO would make him do extra pushups every time he got a letter. Besides the fact he was getting in trouble, he didn't want to read them anyway. Once again, the child bride was crushed. How do I communicate with my husband and try to stay connected unless I write to him?

So here I was married, feeling single, no way to have a relationship with my husband. He didn't write or call. I was ripe for an affair.

****

Yes, when I was 9 years old I was baptized and joined the church. When you're baptized you denounce Satan and you commit your life to Christ. For some people they can go on and live a Christian life and consider themselves Christians.

However, I <u>did not</u> consider myself a Christian. I had an experience with God, baptism, I joined the church, but for me that was far from being a sold out born again Christian. For me being a sold out born again Christian is having a relationship with Jesus Christ. It's reading your Bible, going to church, praying/talking to God and He talks back to you.

During that time in my life I wasn't a Christian and the only life I knew outside of work was bar-hopping. I lived above one why not go to it and the other one around the corner? I could drink and carry on with the men. I was still leading them on but not really doing anything about it. To make sure I didn't do anything about it, I asked my mother or mother-in-law to go drinking and dancing with me. They were happy to oblige. I had a couple of girlfriends my age but they were single. I was a single wife and I knew there, was no point in hanging out in my friend's circles. I had made a choice to be married and I wasn't getting divorced. Not that I wasn't still hoping some way somehow he would divorce me and it would be his fault.

I still hated bars. But I had no other outlet. Bars and hanging out with the family was the only thing there was to do other than stay in that hideous room and hope no one climbed in through the fire escape and killed me.

Side Note: I am very thankful that my husband didn't divorce me in those days. If he had, I would have been married at least 2 or 3 more times. I know I would have married an abuser and one of us would have ended up dead. Probably me. I was on a suicide mission and didn't know how to get off the track. My husband really did preserve me and keep me in a cocoon until I got saved. For that I am thankful.

My husband came home after 11 weeks of boot camp a changed person. I ran to kiss him when he got off the bus at the bus stop, but he told me he couldn't touch me in his uniform. When we got home he didn't want to have anything to do with me physically. Rejection issues were something I dealt with a lot. He was constantly rejecting me in some form or another. It was only by God's grace and mercy, I didn't cheat on him. I wasn't a Christian, but I knew adultery was a sin and I knew if I had sex with someone other than him I would end up pregnant.

When he got out of boot camp and it looked like he was staying in Southern California, he came to get me in Missouri and move me to Oceanside, California. I went from a very small town of 10,000 to a city of 90,000. To say I was totally freaked out and out of my element would be a terrible understatement. He went to boot camp in January, 1980 and moved me to Southern California in August.

We didn't have our own apartment so we were staying with his friends. That was a horrible time in my life. The couple we were living with lived in a one-bedroom apartment and had a baby. The wife had a crush, very obviously, on my husband. In fact, one day when he was at work the woman and her friend ganged up on me and told me he didn't love me and I needed to just go back home. They really put me through the emotional ringer that day. I was barely 21 years old. They were so cruel. When I told him how they acted he didn't believe me. Typical of him, he would always side with someone else.

Before we moved into our own place several of us couples were sitting around the table drinking and talking. A guy knocked on the door who wanted to tell us about Jesus. I remember thinking to myself, "Hot dog, finally someone is going to tell me how to get this hole filled up in my heart." We agreed that the guy could come back later and give us a Bible study. He came back as agreed, but somehow and I don't honestly know how, there was a pornographic center fold picture lying right at the door as he came in.

The guy saw it and said, "You guys are too bad to get saved." Then he left. I was devastated! I thought how in the world am I going to get this hole filled now.

Finally, My God-Sized Hole Can Get Filled Up

One day a couple came over and the woman said she was a born again Christian. I thought, *what in the heck is a born again Christian?* I had only heard the term once and that was about former President, Jimmy Carter. He said He was a born again Christian, but I didn't know what that meant.

Eventually we got our own apartment. Yes, we had a one-bedroom, filthy apartment. The carpet was orange shag but it had a "lovely" sheen of brown. It was soooo dirty you couldn't even see the roaches in it. But for low income military, that was all we could afford. We had no money to get the carpet cleaned, we didn't have a telephone and we lived on a lot of potatoes.

We had no furniture so we had two giant stereo speakers for chairs and a kitchen lunch-bar was our table. We slept on blankets on the floor, but we were in southern California, far from the cold of Missouri. We got a second floor apartment because I was so afraid of a break in, especially while he was gone.

He had to go on a deployment and the born again girl's husband was going too. She spent the night with me before she went back home to northern California while her husband was deployed. As soon as we were alone, I asked her why she was a "born again" Christian and I was just a Christian. All I knew about religion was if you weren't Catholic, you were a Protestant. But I had no idea what being a Christian was, other than a title for religious purposes.

She explained a born again Christian is a person that has committed their lives to Christ. You are totally sold out to Him and you have a true relationship with Him. I asked her if she would take me to church. She said when she got back she would find "her kind" of church and take me.

I waited for six long weeks for her to come back. She did, in fact, take me to a little Pentecostal church – the pastor's name was Pastor Sinner if you can believe it. My husband, her husband, a baby we were babysitting, and I went to church. I wish I had a picture of myself. I know I wore a flashing neon sign that said sinner. My shirt had a keyhole opening in the bust area. I wore tons of makeup and had my hair curled and hair sprayed.

I walked into that church and "wow" is all I can say. I felt the presence of God in a way I had never experienced before in my life. There was a holy reverence there and I knew that's what I had been looking for. I just kept thinking through the service, *How will I get what they got*? One person spoke in their prayer language. I elbowed my friend and asked, "What was that?" She explained someone spoke in tongues, but out of line because there was no interpretation. Then the whole thing turned messy. During the service her unsaved husband and my husband decided to take the baby to the car. She was fussy and they were bored. The service was going way too long – in their eyes. Just as they were about to ask people to come forward to commit their lives to the Lord, one of the husbands came and got us and said we needed to go. They didn't want to stay any longer and they were leaving with or without us.

That was my first experience with the Pentecostal church. Once again, my friend left to go home while her husband was deployed for a few weeks. So I was hanging out with the neighbor downstairs and smoking pot. The neighbor wanted to go to church; I said I did too. I asked her if she knew anyone that could take us. She said she did and called them.

When Rose showed up to pick us up, all I could think was "Oh no, the Jehovah Witnesses have gotten us." Rose wasn't a Jehovah's Witness but a United Pentecostal. I didn't have much knowledge of United Pentecostals except a friend in school was one and when she went swimming it was in her dress.

Anyway, we went one time with her before Christmas and I thought after a very long service, I was bored and wanted to go home. I decided to go again on January 4, 1981. I'm pretty sure Rose picked my friend and me up and took us to church. At the end of the preaching time, the Holy Spirit was moving – some people were behaving emotionally but some were being moved by the presence of God. At the end of the service when they had the altar call I told the Lord whatever those people have, I want it. I want all of it.

We were in theater seating and I remember the pastor saying if there is anyone here that wants to come forward to do so. I did, but I didn't want to step on toes trying to get to the aisle. The person I would have to crawl over saw me looking at the aisle and asked me if I wanted to go. I said, yes, they moved and the next thing I knew I was kneeling at an old fashioned prayer bench bawling my eyes out.

I saw Jesus hanging on the Cross and I knew I put Him there. I was crying and crying and the next thing I knew my chin was chattering and saying stuff I wasn't saying in my head. People were praying for me and crying and saying, "You're getting it, you're getting it." Getting what? I literally could not speak English. I got up from the prayer bench and I looked to the back and there my husband was. I think I must have told him to come and get me at a certain time.

I went out to the corridor where he was and I couldn't even tell him in English what had happened. He said to me that something had happened so go on back inside. I went back in and tried to talk to the pastors. I wanted to get baptized in water but my English was so broken I could barely express myself. This weird speaking in tongues stuff kept taking over.

In that church unless you spoke in tongues, you weren't saved and you couldn't get baptized in water. I now know that was ridiculous, at the time I didn't know any better. As time went on I did get baptized and I stayed at that church a few months.

The problem was they were very ritualistic. If you wore makeup, cut your hair, wore pants and jewelry, you weren't right before God. So whenever the church had an altar call I would go forward and beg God to tell me to quit wearing pants. I had already given up the makeup of a Jezebel, and I wasn't wearing jewelry but I didn't really have very many skirts and dresses so I had to go to the Goodwill to buy clothes. One day I heard the voice of the Lord in my Spirit say, "Don't wear pants anymore." Finally, I had arrived. No makeup, no jewelry and now I wore no pants. I was so self-righteous. I would see women wearing pants and I would say to myself, "Look at them being so nasty their private parts are showing." Really, I mean really, they were wearing slacks or jeans – no parts were showing.

I wore some awful wrap-around skirts, knee high socks and tennis shoes. Yup, sure was pretty pathetic – but I was saved and I was holy! That's all that mattered. Around that time, I noticed that Jimmy Swaggerts' wife, a well-known evangelist at the time, cut her hair and wore makeup and I knew she was saved. I saw other women that I knew were saved doing the same thing and I started thinking – I don't look holy, I just looked stupid.

So I prayed again and told the Lord – Please tell me I don't have to wear skirts anymore.

Then I heard the voice of the Lord say again, "You can wear pants."

I then asked "Lord, why did you tell me to stop wearing pants?"

I promise you as plain as day this is what He said, "I got sick of hearing you telling me to tell you to stop wearing pants so I told you to stop wearing pants." This wasn't an audible voice; it was just a knowing in my heart.

Since I was a young Christian and a people-pleaser like I was, I wanted to do whatever God wanted me to do but I also wanted to do what I felt like the church wanted me to do.

After I got saved I asked the Lord for two things. Give me a baby or take the desire away, and help me to see Chris (my boyfriend from high school) once more so I could tell him about the Lord. He was a heavy drug-user, I knew if God didn't intervene he would die and go to hell. I still loved this man deep into the depths of my soul. The thought of him dying and going to hell was beyond my comprehension.

Around September 15th 1981, I got pregnant. We had tried for 4 years to have a baby even did fertility testing and the doctor said we would never have children. Our body chemistry just didn't work well together and it was impossible for us to get pregnant. I now have that son and two grandsons.

I know what day I got pregnant because I had gone home in August and was gone for about one month. I got pregnant the night I came back.

Through the years as I was living my life the Lord would say to me, "Pray for Chris, pray for him RIGHT NOW!!!!" I'm talking about gut wrenching intercession many, many times throughout 14 years of my life.

I would often ask the Lord if I could find Chris and tell him about the Lord and He would always say, "No not now." My husband at the time and I split up on April 1st 1995. That day the Lord told me, you can find Chris now. I was living in California and the internet virtually did not exist. If it did I wouldn't have known how to use it. I knew that Chris had lived in a small town in Cyril, Oklahoma when we were teenagers. So I tried to find the telephone number for the Chamber of Commerce in Cyril. His family was prosperous so I figured if there was a Chamber of Commerce they would probably know the family.

There was no Chamber of Commerce, but a town hall. I called the town hall and talked to a girl that knew him from school. She said she didn't know where he was, but his family had moved to Anadarko, Oklahoma. A freind and I found the phone number for that last name in that town. I was too afraid to call and find out if he was married so I asked my friend to call. She talked to his stepmother which was more than happy to tell us about what happened.

Chris had gotten into some trouble. He was divorced and had one child. She said he was in prison for one year for drugs. I thought okay, one year I can do that. If we're supposed to be together after all these years (20 to be exact) then I was going to find him. I asked her to ask him the next time she talked to him if I could contact him. She said she was sure he would like to hear from me. She gave me his address and I formed a plan. I knew his birthday was sometime around the middle of April and Easter was late that year.

I got him an Easter card and a birthday card. I wrote to him, reminded him who I was and sent him my testimony about how I got saved. This is the God thing. Chris got my cards ON HIS BIRTHDAY. He had just told the Lord, "I want to serve You, but I can't. I can't do this alone." Then low and behold here I am, telling him I'm saved and I want to help him.

When I got his return letter, he told me what happened. I thought Jesus for sure had a plan for our lives and that Chris would serve his one-year term and be free. It turns out he was in for 20 years for attempted murder of a female. I was devastated but I wasn't giving up. I believed God could do a miracle and get him out of that prison.

We corresponded regularly and he would tell me many, many times that in his past he would be drunk or high, he didn't know how he woke up alive. He should have been dead. I told him the reason he wasn't dead was because God would intervene on his behalf and tell me to pray for him. I know my prayers preserved him.

Chris and I corresponded for about a year. Then it came time for him to make a choice to serve God and live, or rot in prison. I wrote Chris a final letter, crying my eyes out as I wrote it because I knew he wasn't going to follow through with his promise to serve God. I pleaded with him to really sell out to God. He wrote me back one last time and told me he couldn't. It was just too hard in there and he was in survival mode.

I told the Lord it was virtually impossible for me to stop loving him. God had to do it if He wanted me to let him go forever. I was willing to move to the state where he was and fight every day of my life for his freedom. I loved him that much.

All the love that I had carried for that man for more than 20 years just went away. One day when Ann and I were out walking I felt all that love go into a helium balloon and float away. The enemy tried to bring things to my mind, such as what could have, should have, would have happened, if only Chris had made that choice to serve God. He didn't and I will never know what happened to him. It's been another 20 years now since I spoke to him and I'm guessing he's either dead or he got out of prison. It's important to tell that story for a couple of reasons. One is the power of calling out to God and saying "God, I need help down here. I need a Jesus with skin on." God will come through in a miraculous way. Second, I had a choice to obey God or not. I could have moved to that state, I could have been a jailhouse bride and I could have ruined my destiny. What I couldn't do – stop loving this man for my whole life – God could do in an instant.

***

My born again friend and I eventually moved to military housing. We were just a few blocks from each other and we did everything together. We were very close and we were going to church. We would literally yell at people walking through the base housing and ask the girls if they wanted to go to church with us. Sometimes our car wasn't big enough to drive everyone there.

Her mom came to visit, we told her about the church, and she told us to get out of it. Their behavior was ungodly. So we went back to Pastor Sinner's church. He had retired and Sister Mackin and her husband were the pastors. I so loved her, because she loved Jesus and she loved us. After she retired and several years after I had been living for the Lord, I found her telephone number and I called her. She was pretty old at that time and didn't really remember me, but I told her I had gone to her church and I was still saved and serving God. She said the sweetest thing, she said I was "fruit that remained." I think she needed some encouragement at that point in her life. I will see her again one day in heaven and I can see us walking arm and arm on the streets of gold talking about what God used us to do during our time on earth.

I had the opportunity to visit my friend's family in Northern California. During that trip, I had an interesting conversation with the Lord. I knew that I had pretty low self-esteem until I had this conversation with Him. Let me interject here, when I talk about having a conversation with the Lord it's not an audible conversation. It's just a knowing inside of me. The Bible says, "My sheep know my voice and the voice of a stranger they will not follow." I have always had a unique relationship with the Lord and for that I'm thankful.

While on this trip up north the Lord said to my heart one day, "You're calling Me (God) a liar."

I said, "No Lord, I would never call you a liar."

The Lord said, "Every time you tell someone about Me (Jesus) and say that if they were the only person on earth I would have died for them – you wish that was true for you."

I was shocked. I didn't know what to say. Was my self-esteem that low? He continued to minister to my heart.

Theologically or scientifically speaking I don't know when you become a living being with a spirit. I also don't know how a spirit is created. Is it possible that spirits are in heaven waiting for bodies so they can come to earth? I don't know about that – that seems so farfetched to me. Maybe when you are conceived, God makes a spirit and that makes you who you are. I'm too uneducated in the things of the scientific and spiritual world to know when life begins or if life begins at conception. I know that my self-esteem was so low that I subconsciously believed that somehow a wayward spirit, managed to get a body, and land on planet earth. Somewhere in my mind I was so pitiful and pathetic that I didn't even think God loved me.

Now you know why I told the story about my mom and how I was conceived. In 1959, it was unheard of to get pregnant by a man you weren't married to. The proper thing to do was to get married and pretend you got pregnant on your wedding night. In this case since they were both legally married to other people, that wasn't going to happen. It was scandalous to be an illegitimate child. It played into my low self-esteem.

When my born again friend and I returned from northern California, we went to various churches. We couldn't seem to settle on one that we wanted to commit to. We tried some really crazy churches. We went to one church, now this is still about 1981 or early 1982. We dressed up like good church women do, we wore panty hose that matched our clothes and tried to also match our shoes. It was a little hard matching an army green dress without wearing army green hose. I think I eventually managed to find a pair though.

We went to this church that was starting in someone's home. It was still the lingering hippie movement Christianity and we weren't really into that. We were more classic Christians. When they said they were loading up in a van with no seats and heading to someone else's house for house church we said, "Ummm, we will follow you." We are in heels and panty hose and were not sitting in a van like a hippie. We followed them long enough to go to the grocery store instead. They tried to call us and get us to go to their church.

We had some other odd experiences at various churches. The two of us never really settled on one. During that time, I got pregnant with my son. My born again friend wanted to have a baby as well but she couldn't get pregnant. All of our neighbors were pregnant or had babies and she wasn't one of them. It was a very hard time in our relationship. I prayed and asked the Lord to give her a baby too.

After my son was born, our relationship totally changed. It's really hard to have a little one and pick up and go and run around at the drop of a hat. You have to keep the baby on a schedule and you have to have everything packed to go. My friend didn't like that so our friendship started to waiver. Shortly after that, her husband's time in the military was over and they went home.

I was heartbroken. The only Christian friend I had who was my best friend was moving away. Social media didn't exist, phone calls involved long distance charges and neither one of us were writers. We knew that eventually our friendship would dissolve. I wonder to this day how she's doing and if she's still serving God.

(You know who you are. If you ever read this book, please contact me. I would love to catch up with you.)

After she left, I continued to go to this little Pentecostal Church of God church. One problem I had was my husband wouldn't let me drive our car to church. We only had one and it was about a 30-minute drive. We didn't have the gas money to drive there 4 times a week and that's how often I wanted to go. So one day I said to the Lord during the service, if you want me to go to church here You have to get me a ride and I want to come every time the doors are open.

Next thing you know, tap, tap, tap on my shoulder. This lady said to me, "Do you need a ride to church?"

I said "Yes I do and this is where I live." She lived not too far from me and it was on the way to church. Every service, 4 times a week for a year she came and got me and took me home. Sometimes I had the baby with me and sometimes I didn't. She was a true blessing and I appreciated her so much.

I went to that church for some time and I really grew in the things of God. We had managed to get a second car. I insisted that my husband let me go to church as often as I wanted.

My Dear Friend Ann and Our Home Church

I was very lonely. My husband wouldn't go to church with me and he was gone quite a bit of the time. We only had one working car most of the time so he used it to drive back and forth to the base. Sometimes he even had to hitchhike because we were so broke and our car was broken down in some form or another.

I started praying and asking the Lord for a friend with a baby. Shortly after that prayer, my husband said he had a new Sergeant that had just moved to base from Texas. He was married to Ann and they had a baby girl. They wanted to know if we would like to come over for dinner. I was reluctant at first. I was a brand new Christian and didn't really want to hang out with what I called "heathen" people. I was ignorant of the things of God and paranoid of the things of the world that I didn't want to be a part of anymore.

I finally said yes. It turned out the husband was a pretty heavy drinker but Ann had settled down because of the baby. The baby was 26 days older than my son. While we were there, I talked to her about babies, Marine Corp life and other things. We decided since we were both lonely and our kids were so close to the same age maybe we could start hanging out together. We went to a pizza place and I told her she could have a beer if she wanted one. She laughed and said "No, tea is just fine." We laugh to this day about how naïve I was. I hadn't been saved that long, but for some reason, I thought all unsaved people drank beer at lunch and all Christians did not drink any alcohol. I started praying for Ann to get saved. I even told her once, that she was going to hell if she didn't commit her life to Christ. She horrified me when she answered me, "I don't care if I go to hell, I'm living in hell now." Then the Lord started doing amazing things. I had a very large 1970's Pontiac Bonneville. My husband was a low ranking private first class and her husband had to be 3 or 4 levels higher than him. They had a whole lot more money than we did. Ann didn't drive so when she needed to go somewhere, and her husband wasn't around, she would ask me to give her a ride. The Lord told me specifically not to take any gas money from her. One day she offered me some gas money. I said, "What kind of a Christian would I be if I take your gas money?"

Another time when her husband was gone, the Lord woke me up at 4:00 a.m. and said, "Wake up and wait." I'm lying there at 4:00 a.m. wide awake and the phone rings. It was Ann. She asked if she woke me. I said, "Nope, the Lord woke me up and told me to wait." She said Valerie was coughing up phlegm. We were such new moms we didn't know half the time what to do with our kids when weird stuff happened. I said, "Do you want me to come and get you and take you to the hospital 20 miles away?" I didn't say 20 miles away but for this writing, I am throwing that in. She said, "No, can you just talk to me for a minute." We talked for a bit and she was ready to go back to bed with Valerie.

I invited Ann to a Thanksgiving dinner at our church and shortly after that dinner, she got saved. She said she had been taught all her life that Christians were liars and no one would help you but your family. Ann saw a difference in me and wanted what I had. She said it made a huge impact on her when I refused gas money, when we so clearly needed the money, and that I was awake when she called at 4:00 a.m. because God said "Wake up and wait." There are several other events that I'm sure led into her seeing Christ in me and her getting saved, but those are the big ones we talked about.

After several months of our friendship, her husband was going to be deployed overseas for 1 year. She was pregnant and he didn't want her in the area we lived by herself. He sent her to northern California to live with her grandmother. When she moved, our kids were just about two years old. During the time she was gone the Lord would say to me "Call Ann, call her right now." It always amazed her unsaved Grandmother that I would call her just when she needed me. We stayed in touch the whole time she was gone.

After the year passed, her husband returned home from his deployment. Our kids were slightly over 3 then and her youngest daughter, Melissa, was about 9 months old. Ann had warned me Melissa didn't like anyone but her and her grandmother. She didn't even like her dad when she saw him for the first time. It worked out through a lot of prayer that Ann and her family got to move right next door in the apartment connected to ours. It was the cutest thing when Andrew, my son, knew that Ann and Valerie were moving back to our area. He would look at that apartment and say, "That's Valerie's house" in his little baby boy voice.

I kid you not the day Ann, Valerie, Melissa and Ann's husband drove into the driveway of that apartment complex it was as if Ann had gone to the store and had come home. No awkwardness whatsoever. It was as if they had never been gone. Our kids who hadn't seen each other in over a year immediately picked up where they left off. Andrew grabbed Valerie's hand and showed her, her room and then his room in our apartment. Melissa, you know the baby that didn't like anyone? She immediately came to me and we loved each other from day one.

Ann and I have lived a lot of years together. We are family. I love her and the girls as if they were truly my biological family and she felt the same. To this day, we're still very close even though we haven't seen each other physically in several years.

Ann and I found our church that we both went to for several years. Our church was 17 people when we showed up. The Pastor had announced the week before that they were going to start a nursery. They only had 1 baby in the whole church. The next week we came with our three kids and we knew that was the church for us.

We were so pathetic in those days. We were young, poor and very on fire for God. Our pastor called us his spark plugs. Most of his congregation came with him from another church. We were the first newbie's.

I remember rather fondly, but so embarrassingly, about one time when we went to church. The church didn't have a building so we met at his trailer park club house on Thursday nights. I had a car that was so beaten up one of the seat springs popped up in my seat. I tore the seat of my pants. But, by golly, we weren't going to miss church. So we snuck in the back and sat in the back. We always went up to him for a hug after church. If we didn't he would track us down and hug us anyway. I told Ann to go and tell him I tore the seat of my pants and couldn't come and hug him. He found me and hugged me anyway.

Ann and I both grew up in bad households. We were so desperate for a family and our church family loved us so much we were in heaven.

Another time, the church was having their one-year anniversary party. We were meeting in a recreation building in the park. We didn't know what you would wear to an anniversary party in a rec building that was a church, so we asked one of the older ladies in the church. She said we should wear our summer frocks. What in the world is a summer frock? We asked ourselves that question as we walked away.

We guessed it must mean a dress. Once again, Ann and I had no money and we really wanted to fit in. Ann had managed to get three dresses for church, two red dresses, and a yellow one. I think I had a few of those awful wrap around skirts left. So she wore her yellow dress, stockings and dress shoes. I wore one of my nasty wraparounds. We get to the party and everyone dressed like a normal person would in May in Southern California; Khakis, summer dresses, etc.

Her husband took us to the party and before the party was over he came and got us and made us leave. We were embarrassed but everyone knew our husbands were unsaved so they just let us go.

We attended church for several weeks in that recreation building at the park. We had to use this really awful room for the nursery. Our three kids and the one kid of the church were in there. That kid would scream so loud. We didn't know what to do with him. Mary, his mom, told us no matter what, she was not coming to get him. She needed to be in church. She was a single mom and she really did need the break from the baby.

Those babies' turned about 4 or 5 and we asked what could be done for them so they could have church, too. They started a preschool Sunday school.

Eventually it was time for our church to get a regular building. We managed to find a warehouse in the industrial section of town. Ann and I were so sold out to the Lord and our church. We knew God was going to do big things there. We toured a building that I think was about 10,000 square feet. By this time, I think we were 30 or 35 people. Ann and I looked at each other in the building and said, "No way, this is way too small." We went and looked at the other building that had to be double the size. We knew that was the one the Lord would give us.

Sure enough, the smaller building became the Children's Ministry area and the other one was the sanctuary. So many, many memories are in those buildings.

My favorite time was when the church was going to do a 5-day conference. That meant children's church for 5 nights. In those days we could start church at 7:00 and maybe, *maybe* be done by 10:00. That was a miserable time trying to teach children for 3 hours at a time. Everyone would be exhausted and to have to do that for 5 nights in row, we would be lucky to get enough volunteers to do it.

The Lord gave me an idea about breaking up all the kids from Kindergarten through 6th grade and put them in 5 groups. The kids would be in one class room for 20 minutes and then rotate. So the kids would have a snack/movie, lesson, object lesson, story and craft. The teachers would get a new set of kids and the kids would get to do something else and get their squiggles out in between rotations. The teachers also got a 20-minute break with no kids at all. That week we didn't have any rooms for the classes so someone hung tarps for us in the smaller of the two warehouse buildings. We literally rotated those kids from one tarped area to the other. Every 20 minutes whoever was in charge for the night got a bull-horn. I can still hear it over 25 years later, "It's time to rotate." We had an absolute blast. By 10:00 p.m. everyone had been through every tarped group so they sat together in a group and watched a movie.

It was amazing, because every 20 minutes when you got a new group of kids you would have a new anointing and a new way to teach.

I loved those conferences because God came through. I always wrote the curriculum; I would tell Ann the theme and sure enough the Lord gave her the craft for all five nights. I wasn't crafty, but she sure was.

Our church also celebrated Halloween by calling it Hallelujah Night. That was my very favorite time of the year. The kids, Ann and I, would dress up like Bible characters. The first year Ann and I were given a pumpkin skit. One was a sad face pumpkin and the other was a happy face pumpkin. We did the skit where the sad faced pumpkin got saved and then the candle of their heart was lit – we lit the candle inside the pumpkin and turned it around and said, "Now I'm a happy face pumpkin, too." We got so many people saved.

We did that skit a couple of times and the religious people said no more pumpkins. So we did puppet skits several years, and once again someone always got saved. Eventually, our Hallelujah Nights got more sophisticated when we did an old west town. We had all these booths where people could go and play games, buy food, etc. We absolutely loved it. We gave our kids tickets and they ran the gamut at the event. They were in elementary school, but we felt safe and many people knew our kids. They checked in and Ann I would eat our yearly caramel apple waiting for our turn to do a skit of some kind.

One year the Lord gave us the idea of setting up a booth like a bistro setting with a theater stage. Ann and I did a skit about a girl having her birthday party. All she got was a lousy heart. She was so materialistic and she couldn't believe anyone would give her a paper heart for a gift. Then the girl got saved and she was very happy. We led many, many people to the Lord through that skit. Some of the times when the plays were being performed, people had crackers and hot cider. Our skit did the best.

Our church always did a baptism on the 4th of July in the ocean at the Oceanside pier. Pastor would catch mahi-mahi all year and do a fish fry. Everyone brought food. Ann, her husband and kids, my husband and son would be at the beach from the rising of the sun until midnight. We had so much fun.

I have many memories of that church. I wish I could tell all the stories but then this book would only be about my wonderful memories with Ann, her girls, and Andrew, my son. But I must move on with the time line.

Dear God, I'm Divorced

My husband and I were miserable from the start. After we moved to California, I really didn't have anyone but him. My friend that had led me to the Lord was gone a lot. She left when her husband left. Then, of course, they eventually moved.

Before I met Ann and her daughter, I would beg for my husband to spend time with me. His favorite remark was always, "You want me stuck under your crack 24 hours a day." Well yes, part of that time I would like for you to spend time with me and act like you at least "like" me. Frankly, we didn't like each other. We were committed, maybe more because of the son we had or because it was easier that way.

I committed my life to Christ on January 4, 1981. I prayed for 9 years for my husband to become a Christian. I didn't change immediately, no one does. But I did try, after I was saved, to be a good wife. We both made poor choices and equally failed.

Finally, I had had enough and on December 31st, 1989 I found a chair at church and got on my knees and prayed for him to be saved. We had had a good church service and the pastor said if anyone wanted to stay and pray in the New Year they were welcome to.

When I kneeled at that chair I meant business. I cried my heart out to God and begged him to save my husband. I told Him I was willing to allow anything He wanted to do to get him saved, but he needed to be saved immediately. I couldn't go on any longer with an unsaved husband and I was at my very wit's end.

The next day my husband admitted he had called a woman that he was interested in on Christmas Day. When he went out that day he said he wanted to get some air and took my son to a convenience store for a treat. He was actually calling her to talk. I was devastated, to me it was the same as if he had gone down to her apartment and they had had sex.

I cried and cried and talked to my Pastor's wife. She said I needed to ask him if he wanted to be married to me. If he didn't, then he needed to move out so we could get a divorce. Dilemma, my son is in a private Christian school, I am working part time and I didn't know how in the world I was going to support us. But I knew God would provide.

A year before this happened a minister had come to our church and said if anyone was having marital problems come forward and he would pray for you. When I finally dragged myself up there, he touched the palms of my hands and said, "You're going to get a miracle." I said, "Sure, to divorce him."

After the incident with the phone call we had a few more blow outs and decided yes, let's get a divorce. He moved in with a friend but started missing his family. He asked me if he could come home and I told him no. He needed to get saved and move back to Missouri and leave me alone. God was going to give me a new husband as soon as my divorce was final. He wanted to know if I was seeing someone else, I told him that was ridiculous because I was saved and still legally married. I couldn't date someone else while being married but I was ready for the future.

My husband came over one night and said he had gotten saved. I said, "Good for you, we'll see."

The next day the Lord did a miracle. He said, "Bring him home because he can't make it without you." I'm telling you it was like it should have been when we first got married. We really loved each other and enjoyed each other's company. He started going to church and even became the Teddy Bear mascot. If people would have left him alone, in that works oriented church we went to, he would have been fine. But instead, because he couldn't say no, they had him doing something every service. He never sat down, he was the mascot, parking lot attendant, driver to take money to the bank, usher, you name it he was doing it. No men ever discipled him.

He was anointed to do one thing, be Teddy. I can tell you just as clearly as anything he was that Teddy. When he put that thing on he became a new man. The kids adored him. There was another guy, Lion of Judah, same thing happened to him. The church worked him so hard and never discipled him and they both quit serving God. To this day, 20+ years later, he hasn't served God since. They were so much the mascots when they left the church the kids never liked anyone in those costumes again. They actually had to give them away. The two people that were anointed to be mascots, were run over by a works oriented environment.

He continued to go to church and "try" for five years. At the end of that time, he was backslidden, meaner than ever, and back to chasing the woman from five years before. Back to the fighting, crying, screaming, begging for attention.

This time after I talked to my Pastor's wife, she said to give him an ultimatum. Go to church with me one time a week and counseling and I'll go bowling with you. That's where he spent every single Friday, Saturday night and many week nights and that's not an exaggeration. He basically lived there.

I told him on October 15, 1994, that he had until January 1, 1995 to agree to that or be divorced. I fasted, prayed, cried, cajoled, and tried to make a deal until the end of the day January 1. He said he wanted a divorce. I needed him to say those words so I could be scripturally divorced. I tried everything I could, I asked him to move out April 1st. He did. I didn't file for divorce until October. I guess I kept thinking somewhere in the back of my mind he would change his mind.

My son was about 13 at the time we decided to split up. He took the separation and divorce really hard. Christian families didn't split up. He was so mad at God and me that he started acting out of rebellion. He started physically pushing me around and telling me he was in charge of the house. I couldn't get him to follow any of my rules and I couldn't get him to go to school.

The abuse got so bad I called my ex-husband one day and said you have to take him. He's out of control. He went to live with his dad and I was heartbroken. The child I had prayed and asked for, the baby that I knew God gave me, now rejected me. I told the Lord I literally could not bear the pain of that separation. The Lord dropped a scripture in my heart about the Prodigal Son. He said your son will eat slop with the pigs, but he will come home one day. I truly believed my son would be young enough to move back in with me one day. Unfortunately, it was about 8 years after the divorce before my son was willing to hear my side of the story. He had only heard one side, the devastation of what I had done. There are always two sides to the story.

I hoped my husband would change his mind alright. After I filed for the divorce he lost his mind. He threatened me to the point that I had to threaten to turn him into the police. Stalking had become a felony in California at that time. A couple of movie stars had run-ins with rabid groupies; I think one person was actually killed. Because of that, the state instituted a felony charge on stalkers.

My husband started stalking me. My son told me later he would show up at my apartment at midnight, climb a tree with binoculars and watch for me to come home. I had been at church working with my team of children's church workers. We would work long into the night on Saturday to put on a great lesson for the kids on Sunday.

That is still a hard thing. I don't know much of my son's teen years, and quite frankly, I can hardly bear to hear the stories. Apparently they were homeless 2 or 3 times for long periods of time. They had no money and my son quit high school before he ever started. All of that is a part of our journey. I comfort myself with the fact that one day, when we're in heaven together, we won't even remember the years we spent apart.

After the divorce, when my son lived with his dad, I dove head first into doing everything at church. If the doors were open, Ann and her kids and I were there. We didn't know anything else but the church.

After the separation and divorce I was desperately lonely for a male friend. My work in the children's church department was no longer enough and I needed more. I'm not sure what was going on with Ann at that time, but I just needed that male friend.

I knew however, that I couldn't have a man friend, because I would probably get a crush on him and think we were supposed to get married. My choir director, Lory, was married to Rick. The two of them had a best friend, Teri. Teri was a single mother with 3 kids and Lory & Rick had become like surrogate parents to the kids and a team parent with Teri.

I didn't know Rick & Lory very well. But I had joined the choir because I so needed a different social outlet. We all laughed about how bad a singer I was. In fact, to prove this point, is when we were going to do a Christmas play called Come Unto Ye All. It was a cowboy version of the Christmas story. We were rehearsing behind the quilted curtain and I was singing when this voice came from the sound booth, "Bridget, we can hear you singing; be quiet." It didn't hurt my feelings because we knew I was in the choir for the social interaction. They needed me to be in the choir and lip-sync the words, because they needed warm bodies in the Choir.

One day after I had been praying for a male friend, the Lord dropped it on my heart to ask Lory if I could go out with them sometime, and if so, would she invite me to go. They went out quite often after church and loved to run around and do stuff on the weekend. She thought about it for a minute and said, "Sure, we're going out tonight." I then had my male friend with no fear of anything going weird with it because he was married. Rick and Lory are my family. We were all the same age, but for a time it was like they were my parents. We were the three musketeers. When you saw them, you saw me. We had some fantastic times.

One time we loaded up in their Cadillac and decided to go to Mexico for the day. It was Memorial Day weekend. We had lunch, we walked around and when it got dusky we knew it was time to get the heck out of dodge. Rick said specifically to me, "When we start to cross the border, keep your face forward, don't look out the windows and don't point. They'll think we are wealthy Americans and they will attack the car with their stuff to sell."

Well, I listened for 1/2 a minute. I accidentally pointed at this door someone was selling and "wham" they were on us. We bought piggy banks, blankets – in fact after all these years I still have my heavy Mexican blanket. Rick said, "Bridget, I told you to be careful." It was fun. However, the piggy banks disintegrated as soon as we got home; they were so poorly made. I think the only thing that survived was that Mexican blanket.

My life was good, but then I had a major turn of events. I started having a nervous breakdown. I was madly in love with someone and knew beyond of a shadow of a doubt that God had a plan and future for us. We had become very, very close working together in children's church. The anointing and the ministry that was between us was spectacular.

This is a sad and painful portion of my story. Yes, a lot of my life was sad and painful. But there's nothing like being totally and completely in love with someone that rejects you, just to come back later and say, "I missed it, I missed God. You were supposed to be my wife, but I couldn't get past an issue with you." Not only was my destiny changed forever by that sad turn of events, but who knows who else's life was hurt or possibly destroyed by choices that were made.

Like I said before, I was totally involved in church. I

loved being there, being a part of the family and doing whatever was necessary. One day my pastor's wife called me and said our children's church director needed some help. She wasn't sure what he needed, but he needed help and she wanted me to help him.

I was an Administrative Assistant in my full time job. My main function at the church was teaching children's Sunday school. She knew somewhere in the mix of my skills I could help this person that was taking over the children's ministry department. Previously, the Pastor's wife was the children's church director and she was asking this person to take over that role.

I didn't like this particular person. He got on my last nerve. He was short, wore glasses, almost totally bald at the age of 32, and very high strung and quite nerdy. I called him to let him know our pastor's wife had asked me to help him and I wanted to know what he needed. After I talked to him, I felt in my spirit that he had indeed been praying for help and that I was an answer to his prayers. He wasn't very organized and he was a bit scattered in his thinking. He, too, was working full time, but he had a heart for the children.

We built a team of children's church workers, people that either were continuing to teach Sunday school or had a desire to teach Children's Ministry. We had children from kindergarten through sixth grade all in one room. The goal was to teach the kids when the adults were having church. Because the church had two church services, our first service was Sunday school for the kids and the second service was children's church.

In a short amount of time, I could see Joe totally loved the kids. We had so much in common. Joe's core planning group was Joe, his best friend and me. Every night we were working on curriculum for the next Sunday and every weekend we were up until late hours on Friday and Saturday night getting ready for the following Sunday morning. Joe couldn't get his act together enough to have a few weeks of services planned ahead. So we were throwing everything together at the last minute. Over time we started talking about future goals and dreams. Working together and creating what we called "Sunday school in a box." Our goal was to go to struggling churches and bring them a Sunday school. Complete with ideas for props, curriculum, everything you would need to start a children's ministry, from scratch.

While working with Joe and the children's church department, I was praying for my husband to manifest. One day after some event Ann said to me, "I believe the Lord told me Joe is your husband." I had some really deep feelings for him and I knew she was right. I knew he had feelings for me as well, but my weight was an issue. At the time I didn't know it was as big of a deal as it turned out to be.

Joe and I continued to do everything together. To the point Ann hardly ever saw me. She was disappointed in me. I was in love and immersed in Joe and what he needed, I was losing myself. Any time we weren't together we were on the phone talking about another thing we needed to do. You would have thought we were together and we were truly building a life.

I distinctly remember one night he asked me to save him a seat at church. In that church, single guys and girls didn't sit together until they were "dating." This night Joe asked me to save him a seat. I was sitting about the 2nd or 3rd row back. Joe came up and sat down right beside me. I saw the look on my pastor's face. He saw what Joe's intentions were, maybe even more than what Joe wanted to admit.

I was about 50 pounds overweight. I was working on getting my weight off, but I was a junk food addict and was really struggling. I kept praying for Joe and asking the Lord to show him that I was called to be his wife. One day I actually told him that I believed we were supposed to be married after my divorce was final. I was still in the waiting period for my divorce to be final. His response was he couldn't think about that because I was still "technically" married.

Joe and I continued to work together and spent basically every waking moment together. If we had parties, or children's church events, we were together. My heart was so in love with him; my dreams and visions were entwined with him and a life together.

One day during choir practice Joe walked into the room and I started crying. He had gone to hair club for men, got new hair and got rid of his glasses. I had learned to love the nerdy bald guy with glasses, not this gorgeous guy with hair and a great body.

I cried because I was so hurt. It was more important to Joe to be hot and attractive to women than it was for us to build a children's church department, Sunday school in a box and a life together. I didn't know it in the natural, but in my heart I knew something was up with him.

He started hanging out with the "guys" after work. He didn't drink alcohol but he went to happy hour with them. He began making excuses why we couldn't get together and work on children's church material. He was becoming distant. Around that time, I had started working in the same office with Joe. I'm sure that helped a lot for me to see the truth about him and to finally push me over the edge to that nervous breakdown I was having.

Before Hair Club for Men, his chief operating officer didn't know he was alive. Afterword, she really noticed him. She started flirting and carrying on. That's why he was going to happy hour and doing some of the things he was doing.

The day when it all came to a head, she came to church. I remember we were supposed to be doing a skit together during children's church and all I could do was stay in the room and sob. He was sobbing about how good God was, I was sobbing because I knew she was a Jezebel out to take him from his ministry call. If he wasn't supposed to be my husband, fine, but at least continue to head in the direction of becoming a children's church pastor.

Rags to Righteousness

They were together all the time. She was a backslidden Christian that wanted to get right with the Lord. Weird thing was, the Lord wanted to use me to get her back in right fellowship with him. However, Joe wouldn't allow us to become friends. He forbade her from becoming too close to me. True, she was a threat to me and my relationship with Joe. But more than anything she was a woman that needed to be discipled, not loved and isolated by Joe.

I was spiraling into the nervous breakdown I was having because Joe wanted me to meet the spiritual/soul need he had, while wanting her to meet the physical/body need he had. The Lord continued to tell me various things about their relationship. To the point the Lord said this to my heart, "The first time they have sex it will be over." They weren't going to have sex until they got married. They continued to carry on until I was losing my mind, heartbroken over what was happening with her - what was happening to us.

In July, we made the trip to camp meeting, which is a story coming up, and that's when I got the call to go to Rhema. I had to get away from Joe and what was happening. I was keeping my distance from Joe, but the pastor and his wife finally had to tell him to leave me alone. He kept coming back to me and trying to get me to have a relationship with him. I told him I wasn't going to be his administrative mistress and I wasn't going to allow him to drain me of everything spiritually.

As my story goes, I moved to Tulsa in August. Joe and his 'fiancé' came to my going away party and I was pretty much in an okay place. I had accepted he wanted her and everything she had to offer. I had paid the ultimate price by not getting my weight off. He had no character and no patience to wait and see me transformed by my weight loss. He wanted what he wanted.

Now I have to interject here; I knew the price I was paying by not getting the weight off. I chose to allow food to be my drug of choice. I own that. I own the fact that I didn't let Joe fall flat on his face in every bad decision he made. If he fell, I was there to powder his bottom. Love will do amazingly stupid things to you.

After I moved to Tulsa, I heard that Joe was getting married. I remember the movie came out, 'My Best Friend's Wedding.' My Rhema roommate and I went to see the movie. I cried; I was hurting over Joe, but I had to pull myself together.

In March, Joe came to Tulsa for business. He called me, he had been drinking and he said it was over. They got married at Thanksgiving, by Christmas they were separated. He said he told her one night, "You don't love me."

She said, "How can you say that? I married you."

He said, "I know how it feels to be loved by a woman and it doesn't feel like this."

He asked me during that conversation if I thought we were still supposed to be married. I told him he was already married, that I would pray for their marriage to be restored and that I couldn't answer that.

Joe went back to California and I didn't talk to him again for about two years. Joe called me and we had that conversation the Lord had told me that I would eventually have with him. During the call he said he had made a terrible mistake. Their marriage did end within 3 months of their wedding day. His dream of being married and having a family had fallen flat. He said we should have gotten married, we should have had Sunday school in a box and had the baby that I knew in my heart we would have had. He said he did love me but he just couldn't deal with my weight issue. It was a form of vindication for me, but terrible sadness because I still loved him at that point.

Time goes on and I saw Joe one more time. He was not serving Jesus and he appeared to be in a terrible time in his life. The Lord spoke to my heart and said I wouldn't ever see him again.

I did eventually hear that he gained a lot of weight, his

hair was gone and he looked very bad. For a minute I thought *Serves you right, you brat.* But then when I'm right with the Lord I feel sorry and sad. I hope he went on to marry again and have the family he always wanted.

Hillbilly Trip to Oklahoma

In March of 1997, Lory had asked me to go to Kenneth Hagin's camp meeting with her in Tulsa, Oklahoma. First of all, I didn't even know what camp meeting was and I barely knew who Kenneth Hagin was. I had a decision to make regarding my summer vacation. I had the option of going to my 20-year high school reunion or going to camp meeting with Lory.

I talked to my roommate at the time and asked her what she thought I should do. Lory started asking me to go on this trip with her in March. It was now coming up on June and my vacation time was in July. My roommate said to me, "What is going to impact your life more? Going to your 20-year class reunion and seeing people you will probably never see again, or one week of church services?"

Well, that answered my question. I knew going to camp meeting would mean a whole lot more to me than going to a boring class reunion. Lory and I then made plans for our trip.

However, unbeknownst to either one of us, Lory's son had prayed that he could go to Camp Meeting as well. He was about 12 years old at the time. While he prayed we made plans. We'd fly to Tulsa, rent a car and the two of us would have a wonderful week of church.

Then plans started to change. A friend of theirs had just bought an older Mercedes he had the engine rebuilt. Lory jokingly asked him, "How would you like to put a few thousand miles on your new engine?"

He said, "Sure, go ahead."

The son told us that he had been praying that he could go too. Well, we decided 'Okay we have a car to drive. Why not all of us go'? It was going to be Rick, Lory, their two sons and me. We would drive and have a grand old time. Two days before we were to leave, they found out the car we were going to take had a broken air-conditioner. No one had the money to fix it, plus the car was way too small. We couldn't get all of our stuff in the trunk and it would have been miserable for me and the two boys to ride in the small back seat.

Lory's mom had a pickup truck with a camper shell on the back. The camper shell was set up as a raised bed so you could put stuff in the storage. It would be 3 people in the front and 2 in the back who could sleep. The 3 adults could take turns driving so we could drive straight through to Tulsa. Lory asked her mom if we could borrow the truck and she said yes.

Lory called her mom on Friday to tell her we would be there later that day to get the truck. Lory's mom said, "I would love to go with you."

She said, "Mom, if you want to go you are welcome to go." Our plans were made for the trip, everyone got off work and we were excited to get to camp meeting.

Well, I had no idea what was happening. I called Lory from my desk. I wanted to tell her I was on my way. She told me her mom was going and we got more excited. She would be a wonderful addition to our group.

One of the guys I worked with, who happened to go to our church as well, overheard the conversation. He began to berate me by telling me I was horning in on their family vacation. I wasn't the 5th wheel, but I was the toy tire on the car. How dare I do such a thing! I was in tears, and my emotions were totally trashed.

I drove over to Lory's house and I told Teri (Teri is the single mom with three children I talked about earlier) what the guy said. She said, "Wait a minute, this was you and Lory's trip." She confirmed that everyone else horned in our trip. I wasn't the toy tire at all.

We loaded up in the car so we could drive to Lory's

mom's house to pick up the truck and her mom. Everyone was on a very tight budget. It was going to be interesting – but we were going to camp meeting and God would supply – of course.

We drove 24 hours straight to Tulsa. We were hot and miserable, the air-conditioning didn't work right. All you could do, in the back, was ride and sleep. We took turns sitting up front, but because I'm such a poor traveler, I laid down in the back most of the trip.

When we got to Tulsa, we were all squeezed into one Motel 6 room. We were all on a tight budget. But we were thrilled to be here for Camp Meeting. The boys slept on an air mattress, Rick & Lory had a bed and Mom and I had a bed. We made the plan that once we got to the convention we wouldn't leave and go back to the Motel. However, we did end up taking the boys to rest in between meetings.

The first day we were all dressed up in our church clothes. Rick, the gentleman that he is, let us girls sit in the front to stay cool in our nice clothes. Rick was so embarrassed on how we were traveling he told Lory to drop him off down the street. He had to take his suit jacket off because it was soooo stinking hot in the back of the truck, besides the fact it was one of the hottest summers in Oklahoma.

We laugh to this day about how we travelled like the Beverly Hillbillies in that truck. Lory's mom and dad had that truck for several years after that fateful trip.

In between camp meetings on Thursday, Rick, Lory and I were at a fast food restaurant. I had gotten quiet and got up to go to the bathroom. When I came back Rick asked if I was mad at him and Lory for some reason. I said, "No, I'm just about to lose a hip." That was in relation to Jacob wrestling with God and having his hip torn from the socket. I said, "God has called me to Rhema for school. I don't know how I'm going to get back out to Tulsa, with no money and no way to do it, but I'm going to go to school."

Well, they were all excited for me and Rick said that Lory could drive back with me, stay a few weeks until I was settled, and then go back home. That was such a relief. However, I still didn't have money to move or to start school, but I knew I had to go.

We decided we weren't going to tell anyone that I was leaving for Rhema until we had told the pastors of the church. They had said distinctly before we left on vacation, "Don't come back here and say you're called to Rhema." We truly intended to keep it a secret until we got back to Teri's house. I ended up blurting out I thought I was going to go to school at Rhema. Her oldest daughter, Laurie, said, "I'm thinking about going to Rhema too; I need a change."

I said, "Let's go; I'm going."

So in 3 weeks I had to quit my job. She needed to collect her money from an inheritance, buy a car, and we both needed our applications filled out for school. I didn't think the pastor would give me a good recommendation. They told Laurie I was having a nervous breakdown and I wasn't fit to live with. They told her and others some very unkind things about me.

When I heard what they were saying I was devastated. I had loved these people for 12 years and now they're shredding me with their tongues. The Lord said to me "Shut your mouth or it will cost you a year."

We brought an apartment guide with us to California so Lory told Laurie and me where she thought we should live. We rented the apartment full of furniture sight unseen. The plan was for Laurie to pay the expenses and I would eventually pay her back. I'm pretty sure I still owe her some money.

We had a going away party and the hardest thing I ever did was tell Ann, the girls and Andrew goodbye. I had no idea what the next two years would hold, but I do remember telling Ann in a goodbye card... *"I must decrease so your future husband can increase."* Once I know what God has said, I'm like a bulldog. Nothing will cause me to back down or walk away. I may do it kicking, screaming and crying, but I'm going to obey God.

At the end of the three weeks' time, the pastor had filled out our applications and sent them to the school. Lory, Jamison, Laurie, and I packed up our cars. I had barely a carload of stuff in my car. All my worldly possessions were gone. I had given everything to my ex-husband that wasn't personally mine.

As we drove, I distinctly remember Lory asking me if either one of us knew if we had been accepted into the school. I said, "No, but I knew what God said." I was going and I would knock on the door until they told me why I couldn't go or explained what I needed. Laurie had made up her mind if she didn't get accepted she would make sure I got settled and go home. I decided if she got accepted and I didn't then I would stay with her until she graduated.

While on the road, Laurie talked to her mom and found out that she received her acceptance letter. I had transferred my mail to Teri's address, but I hadn't gotten such a letter. It was a Saturday when we found out about Laurie's letter, but I had to wait until Monday. First chance I got I called and yes, I had been accepted as well.

Life at Rhema

When we arrived and got settled, it was time for Lory and her son to go home. I cried and begged Lory to not leave me. I was so hysterical she almost had to slap me. She told me to calm down or I was going to upset Laurie. We had made our choice and in two years we could come home if we wanted to.

I couldn't stop crying. I was so lonely I was beside myself. We both got jobs pretty quickly and started to school in about a week after we got here. But the loneliness was tangible. Laurie is 14 years younger than me and we didn't have a whole lot in common. We were trying to get through school and life for the next two years.

At one point in December, I was so lonely I told the Lord at 3:00 that day, if He didn't give me a friend, today, today - I need a friend or I would pack up and go home tomorrow. It was about 7:00 p.m., dinner break, and I was going to run to QuikTrip for a drink. My co-worker, Olga, asked where I was going and I said to QuikTrip for a drink. I asked if she would like to go and she said yes. She was about my age and single as well. In that 30-minute break I realized she was my new friend. She was the friend I said I needed that day in order to stay in school. God did what He knew I needed Him to do. He gave me a single friend my age.

I used to spend the nights with her so we could stay up and talk and run around doing stuff the next day. I remember one time packing the car to go spend the night with my new friend and I said, "I've got to stop this sleeping around."

Laurie said, "Be quiet, we're Rhema students, they won't understand what you mean." Olga was the dear friend

I needed at that time in my life. I don't know how, but eventually our friendship fell apart, but at that point Rick and Lory had moved to Tulsa for Rick to go to school so I definitely wasn't lonely anymore.

We had some rocky times during the two years that we attended school. We were so incredibly broke it was awful. When we got paid it was a big treat to go to Walmart and buy a few groceries.

Pastor Hagin told us when we were going to Rhema that we had to go to church there. I had gone from basically being one of the founding members of my church and going there for 12 years to this huge church where I knew no one and I was far from being a founding member.

My church had grown to over 1,200 before I left to go to Rhema and Rhema was a church of about 5,000 at that time. I was sad, lonely, and worn out. I pretty much lived in survival mode. I loved God and I wanted to obey Him. I wanted to do everything He had told me I would do one day, but I was too heartbroken.

Laurie and I managed to graduate in May 1999. During school one of the teachers said, "When you graduate, get out of here and go somewhere, anywhere, but don't stay here and become moldy." I took that to heart. I didn't know what to do or where to go so I decided to go back to California. While I was at Rhema, my car got repossessed so I didn't have a car. The plan was for me to buy Rick & Lory's Cadillac, yes the one we had driven to Mexico in. I was transferring my job to San Diego and I was going to stay with Teri until I got on my feet. Everything was set, the job transfer was done. It was a Tuesday before I was to leave on Friday. The Cadillac got totaled. Now I had no car to drive. The Lord had also dropped it in my heart to leave all my stuff in Tulsa. I would go out there and come back in August to get my stuff after I found a place to live.

Not to be deterred, I couldn't take my stuff, the car was totaled but by golly I was going to obey God. I bought a bus ticket to San Diego. Wednesday night I had a dream that my dad knocked on my door and said "How does it feel not to have a mother?" It was 4:00 a.m. I woke up Laurie and said, "My mother is going to die, I have to see her one more time before I move. Can I borrow your car?"

She said, "Yes of course." I made the long drive to Missouri. I saw my mother, asked her if she was ready to meet the Lord. I saw my sister and told her mother had made her peace and was ready to go. I told my sister that our mother would live forever and I drove back to Tulsa.

Friday morning at 4:00 a.m., Laurie dropped me off at the bus station. I decided to have the bus people take care of my suitcases so I wouldn't have to drag them on and off the bus. As soon as I sat down I knew I had missed God. My stuff was on the way to California, my job had been transferred, I was on the bus and my ride just left. I knew that I knew that I knew that I had missed God and I wasn't supposed to go.

There was nothing to do but go to California, work a few weeks get the money and go back to Tulsa. After 36 miserable hours on the bus, Ann picked me up at the bus station. She said, "I don't know how to tell you..."

I said, "Who died?"

She said, "Your mother."

I had to find money somehow, and I honestly can't remember how, but I had money and got back on the bus for another 36 hours to Missouri. I went to my sister's house. I called my old job; yes, I could get it back and I asked Rick and Lory to come and get me in a week.

In that time, we had my mother's funeral. She had planned it out anyway so we only had to show up. We cleaned out her house and got everything over to the auction house. I spent the week trying to reconnect with my brother and sister, but unfortunately, it really didn't work.

Rick & Lory came to get me and got me safely back to Tulsa.

The point in this series of events is this: You have to

hear from God yourself. You can't let a teacher at school, a friend, a roommate, or anyone else tell you to do something. I'm sure that Rhema teacher meant well. But I was called to stay in Tulsa. I was called to plant some roots here and build a life. But my people pleasing self didn't know that. I only knew that my teacher, someone in authority, told me to get the heck out of dodge, so I tried.

Life After Rhema

Life after Rhema has been good. I finally settled down and allowed myself to really like living in Tulsa. When I first came, I was in a bit of a culture shock. Even though I grew up in a small town in Missouri and remembered the cold, cold winters and the hot, hot summers, I hadn't lived in this weather for 17 years.

In southern California it's the land of the perfect weather. You occasionally worry about an earthquake, but with no humidity, snow, tornadoes or anything else. You can learn to live with an occasional earthquake. In Oklahoma it's everything bad; earthquakes, tornadoes, cold-cold, hot-hot and humid.

But, you have to love the place where God calls you to be. I've lived here since 1997. Over the years I've grown accustomed to the weather, the earthquakes and we just watch the tornadoes, pray and take cover if necessary in our coat closet.

After I graduated from Rhema I was single. I longed to be married. My first marriage was during my whole young adult life. I really liked the security of being married. I was single for 10 years from the time I got divorced until I remarried again on July 8th, 2005.

During that time, I regularly prayed for my husband. I discovered long ago that you have to be specific regarding some things that you're praying for. I didn't want to just "get married" for the sake of having a husband. I wanted the husband God had for me. I prayed and asked the Lord, "What should I ask You for in my next husband?" I got very specific and this is what I prayed for: A man that loves God more than I do. I am willing to pack my bags and move to the jungles of Africa if that's what God asks me to do. I may go kicking and screaming, but I'm willing to go. My husband had to be more willing than that.

I wanted a man that loved me as Christ loves the church. He must love me as he loves his own body. I also found out, really quick, if a man has low self-esteem, he'll never be able to love me as Christ loves the church.

He needed to be my best friend. Remember I said my ex-husband told me "You want me stuck under your crack 24 hours a day." Yes, I sure do. I think a husband and wife should want to be together more than they are apart. Bottom line, I wanted a best friend.

He had to be a tither, giver, 100-fold giver, a man who loved to give to the church.

Finally, he must be a man that was a Godly example of a man for my son.

The one thing I knew for sure when I saw my future husband was that I would know him. It would be as if he had gone on a long business trip or he had been in the military and out on a mission. I had prayed for him and envisioned him in my mind for so long there was no doubt in my mind that I would know him when I saw him.

I didn't date much, but when I did, I tried to make whoever I was dating at the time be the "one." I would meet some guy and try to make myself believe that he was everything I had prayed for. I would pray that the Lord would show me if he wasn't the one and that he would be removed from my life. Every single one of them was not it. I was lonely and getting desperate, but I knew that there would never be a third husband for me. That meant I had better be super careful to make the right decision for number two.

I remember the tears, fits, and the prayers that I made wanting my husband to come into my life. But in reality I wasn't ready for a husband like the one God eventually gave me. I had rough edges, a bit of a hateful attitude and some other ungodly issues that were not fitting for a new marriage.

The Lord had to do a lot of work in me. I was still hurting from the breakup with Joe, if you can even call it a breakup since we technically never got together. I had some hang ups from the past as well. Because of that, I treaded very carefully whenever I met someone new.

In January 2005, the Lord dropped in my heart to join E-Harmony. I had done some internet dating before, but felt like the Lord told me to get off the internet dating websites and just sell out to Him. I had always heard when you stop looking for your soulmate he will show up. Problem was I didn't know how to stop looking until I knew how to stop looking. I know that sounds very odd. I had tried for so long to stop wanting a husband but I didn't know *how to stop* wanting one...until it happened.

I had gone to enough single events just knowing I would meet "him" at one of these events. Who came to the events? A bunch of middle aged, overweight, miserable women. Maybe a few guys, but mostly none. One day I decided enough was enough. I was tired of being lonely on a Friday and Saturday night so I was going to do something to change that. I decided that women friends were good enough.

I started a networking group of single people (mostly middle aged, heavy women) and I looked for things to do every weekend. When I found something I would send an email out to everyone, call my closer friends and make plans. I had decided I was never going to get married so I might as well sell out to the Lord. I was tired of pining away for a man that I figured didn't exist. It was during this time I realized I had finally stopped looking. I had decided that I wanted more of God and I wanted to be obedient to Him no matter what. It didn't appear that a husband was in my near future so I needed to give up the hunt. Remember, I was told when

I stopped looking that he would show up? I finally figured out how to stop looking.

There are 50 Methodist Churches in Tulsa alone. I was working and attending a Methodist Church at the time, so I started contacting other Methodist churches to find out what their single adults were doing for fun. I actually ended up on a committee with the largest Methodist Churches in town that were having a Singles Conference that October. I was getting busy with this committee when the Lord told me to go on E-Harmony, I thought it was a joke.

I called Ann and told her what I thought the Lord had dropped in my heart about E-Harmony. She said, "Well, I was going to talk to you about that; you're supposed to do it." I signed up and got disappointed, like you do on these dating sites. I started out locally, then 50 miles, 500 miles and nationwide. I didn't want a person that drank alcohol or smoked. When I went nationwide I thought it wouldn't be so bad to have a smoker maybe they would quit. That day, April 19th 2005 – I matched with Peter from Jacksonville, Florida. I matched with four other guys, but I never contacted them.

Peter and I went through the whole E-Harmony process in 3 ½ hours. I was at work and he was at the library. He said when he got up from the chair he was practically crippled. I got together with my prayer partner the next night and we were praying over this match that I had with Peter. The Lord gave me a word that let me know Peter was the one I had prayed and asked God for. I wasn't totally sure, however, because Peter and I had some differences that I was concerned about.

I didn't tell Peter about my ministry call and he could have never figured it out on his own. The third night after we matched he told me about a dream he had and the vision of the ministry he believed the two of us had. Sure enough it was exactly my ministry call. Except for one-night, Peter and I talked at least two times a day for hours. We planned our phone calls when our cell minutes were free. We talked for hundreds and hundreds of hours. That's all we could do since he was in Florida and I was in Tulsa.

Peter told me shortly after we matched that we were going to get married as soon as his boots hit Tulsa I told him, "Peter, people just don't do that. We have to date first."

He stood his ground and said, "No, as soon as my boots hit Tulsa, we will get married."

The Lord knows everything. Peter has a childbirth disability that is really hard to detect most of the time. Because we weren't physically together, I didn't really know the extent of the damage. I had prayed and fasted and knew God said Peter was the one for me. We made plans for Peter to arrive on July 7th and we would get married on July 8th. The first time we saw each other would be a Thursday and we would get married that Friday. I had made a firm decision. When I picked Peter up from the airport, if he wasn't the one, I wasn't going to marry him. I didn't know what I was going to do with him, but I wasn't marrying him.

I told him, "See, you're coming on a Thursday so your boots will be here for a day before we get married." Guess what? His plane was delayed. He got here at 3:00 a.m. on July 8th. When he finally arrived and starting walking down the runway, I knew he was it. It was exactly how I knew it would be. When I saw him, it was as if he had just come home from a long business trip. We never had any awkwardness between us. We were "home" with each other immediately.

We got married at 2:30 p.m. in Bentonville, Arkansas. Our first date was our wedding day, just as Peter said, "As soon as my boots hit Tulsa we will get married." As of the writing of this book, we just had our 11th wedding anniversary.

Now I wouldn't recommend any of this to anyone looking for their future mate. What I would recommend is that you pray it out, ask counsel from your friends and don't let desperateness and loneliness be the deciding factor on who you are going to marry.

He's everything I have prayed and waited for. I didn't always wait patiently or well, but I did wait until I got the exact person God had in mind for me.

We are members of Rhema Bible Church and we volunteer on a regular basis as the Lord leads us.

Peter's three sons live in Florida, he has a daughter-in-law and his granddaughter was just born. My son lives in Missouri with his two sons.

We're obeying God in every way that we can, but it's still a rocky road to walk. When two people become one, they really need to understand the differences between the two of them. I'm still a bit on the fearful/negative side and can be a major introvert. Peter on the hand, could literally talk to a rock if it would sit there long enough to listen. It used to embarrass me how he would start talking to random people about his life. I would cringe. Now I'm used to it and I head for the car when it gets to be too much.

But that makes life interesting: to enjoy each other's differences without destroying each other's individuality.

As of the writing of this book I'm working a full time job and writing/blogging on the side. However, the Lord is opening ministry opportunities for us and soon I will be a successful self-employed writer, author, international seminar speaker. You speak those things that are not as though they are.

God has a plan for each of our lives and now that my God-sized hole in my heart is full – I am free to do whatever He asks

There is a Purpose

There is a purpose for this book. Lots of people have stories to tell. Some people have lived a more horrific life than I did. But the point of the matter is this: When you have a God-sized hole in your heart, there is only one way to heal that. That's through a relationship with Jesus Christ.

I knew about Jesus and even called myself a Christian, but until I was confronted with the fact that there's more to being a Christian than a denominational title – It's a relationship with the true and living God - I wasn't fully settled.

I was broken, alone, bleeding inside and couldn't find an answer until that day I was introduced to Jesus Christ. When I saw Him hanging on the cross and I knew my sins put Him there I broke into a million pieces.

If Jesus can take my life that was so broken and messed up, He can take anyone's life and turn it for good.

Today, I'm a writer, teacher and soon to be a seminar speaker. My wounds of the past have healed and I'm thankful to be on an exciting journey with Jesus. I don't know what the next steps are, but once again it's a journey of faith.

I am asking you now – do you have a God-sized hole in your heart? Are you living a sad, depressing life and feel like you're just existing? Or, are you living a life that says – I don't do drugs, I'm not overly sad, I don't really do anything wrong, but there is still something missing. We all come from different walks in life. Maybe you didn't try to fill your emptiness the way I did. Maybe you are so empty inside because you didn't realize there was something missing.

But I can tell you there's a heaven to gain and a hell to shun. The God of the universe wants to come into your life and set you free. There's so much more to life than existence and just getting by.

Won't you join me in asking Jesus Christ into your heart as your personal savior? Repeat this after me, "Jesus, please forgive me of my sins and come into my heart. I repent of all my sins, those that I can remember and those I cannot. I ask you to forgive me and to come into my heart. Thank you Lord, I am now a Christian."

Now that you have said those words, you can be assured that your name is written down in heaven. The angels are rejoicing and dancing that you've made a decision to follow Jesus Christ.

Today you must decide that you're going to live the life, the whole life God sent His son to give you. Get yourself a Bible, attend a good Jesus preaching church, be baptized and buckle your seatbelt and get ready for the ride of your life.

Dreams and Goals

It wasn't until I committed my life to the Lord that I could focus on fulfilling some goals.

I would ask myself, "What do you want to be when you grow up, little girl?" I want to be a schoolteacher because I want to write on the chalkboard as much as I want. I also want to use the chalk holder because that is cool.

What do you want to be when you grow up, little girl? I want to be a sales and marketing person. I want to go to college and marry a college graduate and have a nice big house, with 2 cars and 2 kids.

What do you want to be when you grow up, little girl? I want to be a mommy and stay home and raise my 6 kids.

What do you want to be when you grow up, little girl? I want to be an archaeologist because I want to visit the Great Pyramids of Egypt one day.

What do you want to be when you grow up, little girl? I want to be a secretary like Lucy on the "Here's Lucy Show" and work for a banker like Mr. Mooney.

Everybody has dreams and goals. Well, I should say everyone has dreams and goals instilled in them at birth but not all of them can and will come to pass.

When I was growing up I did have dreams – I did dream about all of those things. But as my life progressed my dreams got stolen. First by my probation officer, yes when I got back home after I ran away from home I was on probation until I was 18. I told her I wanted to be an archaeologist she laughed and said, "That's never going to happen. You have to have perfect grades, a perfect life and lots of money. You have to attend an Ivy League college, so you might as well forget it."

Then my mother, "Your dad is never going to pay for college. You might as well forget it – he's a drunk and a liar and he's never going to do anything for you."

I started asking myself - how in the world would I pay for college? I had no one to ask, no one to talk to, and did not have the slightest clue what I needed to do to have any of the dreams that I had planned for come to pass. But you know how the story goes – I got married at 18 and divorced at 35. However, there is a part of the story that you don't know.

Shortly after my then husband and I moved to California and we had our son, I was really praying and asking God for help with my life. I didn't want to continue to work blue collar jobs. I really, really wanted to make more money and be successful at something. One day I was going through a drawer and I found my grade cards from high school. Now I have to say I am not a packrat. I end up throwing stuff away that I really need, but at the time I think I don't need it.

To found my grade cards after all that time was a miracle in itself. I looked at them and realized I had attended a Vo-Tech school while in High School. My office skills were pretty good and I got decent grades. The dream was rebirthed in me to be a secretary - that's what we were called back in those days.

Problem was, once again I didn't know how to get the correct training for such a job. The internet didn't exist in those days, but I managed to find out about a free night school that taught basic secretarial skills. I attended that school a couple nights a week for a few months. I will never forget my first office job. I was working in an executive suite with about 50 offices. The premise was that I would sit in the lobby and become everyone's secretary. Many offices were around the perimeter of that lobby and I had a huge console phone. So, when the phone rang, I became that company's secretary. I was really good at multi-tasking and was able to keep everyone straight. I loved that job and everyone loved me.

Over the course of thirty years I had a variety of Secretarial aka Administrative Assistant positions. My last Administrative position – I worked at a bank for the Senior Vice President of the bank, no, his name wasn't Mr. Mooney, but I loved working at that job. When I started the job, it was my dream job. When the time came for me to end my career as an administrative assistant I had fulfilled the dream of being like Lucy on the Here's Lucy Show.

I'm now 50+ years old and in October of 2015 I was absolutely sick of my life. I had fallen into a bad trap of working on what I call the chain gang. You get up, go to work, come home, go to bed, and get up and do the same thing over again 5 days a week. Saturday you sleep in, run errands, and go to bed just to get up and spend Sunday at church, eating, napping and going back to church.

I said, "Lord, there has got to be something more to life than this." He had given me a dream and a vision of a women's ministry back in the early 80's. I hadn't been a Christian very long but as plain as day He gave me a vision of a book, a ministry, seminars, teaching/preaching and evangelizing. He even gave me a price per person for the seminars.

What happened between the time that God gave me a vision and October 2015? *Life.* Life took over. Some good, some bad and some plain out ugly. All the time I had a dream in my heart, but it had been covered with hurt, pain, shame, divorce, lack, loss and a new husband. How in the world was the dream of what God told me to do ever going to come to pass?

It comes by getting back on my knees, like I originally did, and asking Him – "Is this all there is? Is this all I'm good for? Bringing home a paycheck that barely pays the bills and hoping maybe on one Friday night you can go out to eat without having culture shock over a $30.00 steak dinner?

There has to be more."

Then I remembered I had heard about dreams/visions and goals from a minister by the name of Terri Savelle Foy. I had seen her book at one of the churches we were attending about a year before but honestly it sounded New Age to me. It sounded so silly to think that you could just dream, have a board with pictures on it and then actually see them come to pass.

But, back in October 2015, she came to mind again. I found her website and started listening to her podcasts. I can tell you she lit me up like a Roman candle. I was so fired up I couldn't believe that I had let a whole year go by and hadn't touched any of her teaching.

She had a conference coming up, in January 2016. I had already made up my vision/dream board like she said, so I told the Lord if He wanted me to go to that conference He would make a way. I told my good friend Denise about Terri and she started listening to her as well. She got lit up and excited too. We made plans to go to that conference. To say it was life changing would be "to say the least."

I started really dreaming, really praying – confessing the Word over my life and then one day it unfolded before my eyes. The Lord hadn't forgotten or given up on me. He still wanted me to have that ministry to women. He wants me to teach women about dreams and goals. We don't have to live on the chain gang and just exist. We can live every dream He has ever given us. We just have to be in the right place to listen.

My friend, Denise, has a similar past like I had with my family. In some ways I think hers was a tad worse. At 60, she felt like she, for sure, had no dreams and no goals. God couldn't possibly use her to do anything – other than work.

But the more we listened to Terri Savelle Foy, the more she believed God had something in mind for her as well. One day she woke up and she saw it. She has a food ministry for shut-ins. Everyone tries to feed and care for the homeless, but what about the people that are at home alone – day in and day out. Sure Meals on Wheels takes them food, but do they stay and pray with the person? Do they take 5 minutes out of the rush to deliver the food to talk to them? Sometimes talking is more valuable than throwing a frozen meal at them.

Her ministry is called 'His Provision' and we're so excited to see it start to unfold. God has a big vision and call on Denise's life that was planted in her at birth. But once again, life took over and she had no idea it was possible.

I have another friend, Amy, as of this writing she has left to pursue her dream of living on the beach in Point Loma, California. She is starting a ministry to the prostitutes and the women that are involved in the sex trade of that area. It's a port city so you know there is a lot of that out there.

I remember when Amy and I started meeting a couple times of month early January 2016. She went from, 'I sure would like to live on the beach, to I want to live on the beach, to I'm *going* to live on the beach.' It was a 6-month journey. God did huge supernatural things to reveal Himself to her and to get her where she's going.

I have another friend that is 65 and I was telling her there was more for her in life than dieting and cooking nutritious food all day. Her children are grown, her husband works long 12 hour days and her mother had passed away. She told me, "Bridget, I don't know how to dream."

Another friend got hit with a very rare form of cancer. Her mode for over 6 months was to get well. But while she was sick, she realized she hadn't really lived. She hadn't done much of anything and had lost her vision and desire for what God had for her.

I could go on and on about the women that I've met that had no dreams/no goals and thought "Is this all there is? Just to work and make a living?"

During the revelation of what God gave me, He also gave me a business. I've always loved writing and I even found a certificate from 3rd grade that was a writing certificate. You know I just said I don't keep anything, but I found that. My dreams were rebirthed and rekindled. My love of writing, my desire to help people, and to realize that we all have dreams and goals just needed to be reintroduced to me.

I started a business called Casting Your Vision, LLC. As women, we spend the majority of our lives care taking and making sure everyone else is okay. We put ourselves on the back burner and then we wake up at 50+ and say "Is this all there is? I have no one to take care of." So you sit down in your chair in front of your television – day in and day out - and you grow bitter, angry and lonely.

We think there is no time left. I can't start doing such and such now that I'm 50+ years old. I mean really how much more time do I even have left on earth? Well, you know people are living longer and longer these days. I saw a picture of an 87-year-old woman that could easily pass for 60's. She's planning her vacation to Hawaii. Age is just a number.

Casting Your Vision, LLC was birthed out of someone who said, "God, is this all there is?"

What are your dreams and goals? What do you want to be when you grow up, little girl? What do you want to be when you grow up, little boy?

Everyone has God given dreams and goals. There is hope even if you're a shut-in. There is hope even if you're in a wheelchair. You can dream and find out what God has for you. There was a woman, Joni Eareckson Tada, that was in a tragic diving accident and she became paralyzed. She could have given up hope and thought, *"This is all there is!"* But instead she has gone on to do tremendous things for God. She may be paralyzed in her body, but she's not paralyzed in her soul and in her spirit.

What are your dreams and goals? What do you want to be when you grow up, little girl/little boy? Chase your dreams, find mentors, even if they are people you listen to via podcast, TV or another media. Dream, *dream big* and chase after those God-sized dreams.

Letter to the Reader

Peter and I are called to the nations, particularly to the African continent. Did I pick the call on my life? No! Would I want to do anything else? Nope! It's hard work and it's walking by faith. I've had a book and a ministry call in my life for over 30 years. Because of circumstances, decisions made and paths crossed, the original ministry call is gone. The Lord said there was no time to develop it now. I was sad, but I understood. Now I walk in the full measure as much as I can.

Not too long ago I tried to faith buffalo God. I was crying about something not manifesting quickly enough and I said, "God I've done everything you have asked me to do, why isn't it here yet?" The answer, "No you haven't because you haven't done 'such and such.'" Busted!!! I knew as I was saying it that I was wrong, but I still said it.

Jesus Christ is the same yesterday, today and forever. No matter what your past looks like, you can face tomorrow. God can take your filthy rags and turn them into a crown of righteousness.

Let me come along beside you virtually. Let me help you find your reason for being and what your Jeremiah 1:5 looks like.

Please read this book and share it with a friend, leave a review on amazon, or feel free to email me at: bridget@castingyourvision.com.

www.ingramcontent.com/pod-product-compliance
Lightning Source LLC
Chambersburg PA
CBHW071530080526
44588CB00011B/1625